It's a Matter of Dominion!

Roderick L. Hennings

ISBN# 9781549510144

DEDICATION

This book is dedicated to my wife for life, Pamela Hennings. Without you, there's no covenant, and my two beautiful daughters: Ariane and Chloé Hennings, you make me necessary!

I love you more than you'll ever know...

"As a man of faith, community and family, Bishop Hennings speaks powerfully and eloquently from the heart and is able to lift up members of our community, despite any challenge they face.

- Mayor Byron Brown of Buffalo NY."

"Bishop Hennings, one of the nation's most exciting preachers, tells his story as only he can. I'm sure it will inspire and captivate you to a higher dimension."

- Bishop J. Drew Sheard, General Board member-COGIC.

"Bishop Roderick Hennings is an extraordinary spiritual leader in western New York, when I need a word Bishop Hennings always delivers! Every time I hear him preach I feel as if he's talking directly to me!"

- Senator Tim Kennedy, New York State Senate.

"Bishop Hennings has keen spiritual insight, and it's wonderful to know the world will experience his ministry!"

- Pastor Benny Hinn, Televangelist.

CONTENTS

ACKNOWLEDGMENTS

Special thanks to my amazing church family- Zion Dominion Global
Ministries in Amherst and Rochester, New York. Thank you for giving
me the privilege to serve you.

Kyle Patterson, we did it!

Ebony Nicole Smith.

To everyone who pushed me to deliver.

1 CHICKEN WINGS AND CHEERIOS

I grew up in the 1960s on the southside of Youngstown, Ohio in a close knit neighborhood. Every parent was every child's parent and every child was every parent's child. My mother worked hard to raise our family. I did all the things kids growing up in Youngstown did. We lived a modest life. I went to public schools there and enjoyed sports. We weren't rich and we weren't dirt poor. I grew up as the youngest of five brothers and sisters. It was overall a decent upbringing. My father was not a part of my life at all.... My mother didn't raise us in church, but she taught us what she knew to be truth.

We didn't have a neighborhood at that time that was full of violence, however, the family structure was dysfunctional. My mother was with my father and my father was married to his wife! So that's how I got here! I wasn't raised in a Christian home, but as God has a way of doing things, Grace raised me (my mom's name is Grace). He got a hold of my heart as a young man and forever changed the course of my life.

I was 17 years old and somewhat precocious, always hanging out with guys older than me. One Saturday night, my cousin Keith Burnett asked me to come to church with him. I asked him if any girls would be there.

He said, "Yeah, sure, some girls will be there." So I agreed to go. I was a social, gregarious young man who enjoyed getting out and trying new things. At the time I had a process, we called it, a hair style down to my shoulders, it was really crazy! So off I went the next day to a little church there in Ohio. I wasn't expecting to have a Jesus encounter or anything, but that Sunday at 341 Jefferson Street I heard the gospel preached in a way that revolutionized my thinking right then and there and transmogrified me, changed me with an absurd effect! That very day I gave my life to the Lord and my pastor, the man that changed my life, Pastor Willie Jerome Wilson would become a father to me in the faith and in life. I heard that man preach the gospel, a simple message and it forever altered the course of my life. It was an incredible experience. And as the old saying goes, "I've been running with Him ever since!"

Pastor Willie Jerome Wilson, took me in as one of his own sons and began investing in my life. He had four sons and one daughter and they welcomed me as part of the family. They became my brothers and sisters. It was an amazing experience. After service I would go to their home and hang out. Growing up in a single parent home, I didn't have an example of a father, and for me I believe you need to see a man to be a man. I had men around me growing up, but intimate time, I just didn't have that. That's what Pastor Wilson became to me. He was an example to me of a man, and showed me how to raise a family and preach the gospel. He lived in Hubbard, Ohio and I would drive out to his house to do chores and he would minister to me about faith.

9

Paul the Apostle said you have many teachers, but you don't have many fathers. No man is a self made man. That idea is nonsense! Every young man needs a father who can guide, direct, exhort, rebuke, and help him become all that God created him to be. To this day I still have a relationship with Pastor Wilson. He retired from the ministry and lives in Alabama, but I brought him to Zion Dominion, the church I lead today in Amherst, New York a couple of years back. He just cried and cried to see all that God had done. I praise God for his deposit.

Back when I was at his church in Ohio, I served in anyway I could. Anything that needed to be done, I was able and willing to do it. I pretty much held every position in the church, except deacon. I was the van driver, the youth director, choir president, choir director, janitor, usher, praise and worship leader, devotional leader. I started teaching Sunday School and that's really where it all started. I became more interested in watching people mature in the faith, rather than just getting a whole bunch of people into the church, though I brought someone with me almost every time I came to church. I began talking to my pastor about my desire or burden if you will, to disciple believers and really see them matriculate in the faith. My pastor recognized this desire as a call of God on my life to begin ministering to people. They called it a trial sermon back then, a opportunity to see what type of potential you had as a minister. It was as though if you didn't do well, you couldn't be a preacher, as funny as that sounds. So I preached my first sermon in 1981 on a Sunday evening. I still remember the message, "Fear knocked, faith answered and no one was there." So that was my genesis in the ministry. Pastor Wilson had a powerful ministry on faith and miracles. He was paralysed from his neck down from multiple sclerosis, and God healed him miraculously! Amazing man of faith. He saw ministry in me and I am forever grateful for that.

So I continued serving in any and all capacities that opened up for me while working at a local hospital. It was a good job, it provided understanding dealing with various types of people who were made vulnerable by afflictions, yet I knew there was more that God had for me to do for Him in ministry. I was single at the time, and an opportunity had opened up for me in California. I had about two weeks left to pack and prepare when the Lord spoke very clearly. It was a simple phrase really, but I knew it to be the voice of the Lord. He said, "Your destiny is in Buffalo!" I had only been to Buffalo one time in my life when I had preached at a youth convention. On one hand I knew I could fit in good in California, but in my heart I knew the Lord calling me to serve him in Buffalo. My heart was to obey my Lord, so it wasn't a question of if I would go or not, but what exactly was in store in Buffalo, of all places? At the time, it was a city in transition. The changing of industries, the decline of manufacturing and the bankruptcy of Bethlehem Steel had left the city in poor shape, similar to Youngstown Ohio! It seemed God was calling me to play a role in rebuilding a broken city by focusing on rebuilding broken lives, hearts, and families. So if my destiny was in Buffalo, I was ready to take the step of faith and follow Jesus wherever he decided to send me. I learned to feel the fear and do it anyway!

I was single for a year living in the B-Lo (Buffalo) and chicken wings and Cheerios made up most of my diet...I learned more about myself and learned the power of introspection! Being alone does not equal loneliness... It became a Matter of Dominion!

Let's pray.

Father, I thank you for the call of God on each of our lives to take up our cross and follow you. For me, it was to lay down the dream of California and come to the city of Buffalo. Lord, as each of us seeks to obey and follow your leading, give us hearts that love and obey you and serve you with all our hearts, souls, minds, and strength. In Jesus' name, Amen.

2 A GROWING CHURCH

I left everything in Ohio, and moved to Buffalo in 1987. I was single at the time, but after a year in Buffalo, I married my lovely wife Pamela, also from Ohio, and brought her with me to Buffalo to join me in the ministry. When I arrived in Buffalo my first pastor was Pastor Lee Allen Spight Sr, pastor of Holy Temple COGIC. I joined his church and I became a son of his in the faith. He really pushed me to be all that I could be in Christ and exposed me to the national church. He gave me opportunities that I could have never had otherwise and opened doors for me. He once again showed me the power of not just teachers in the faith, but of fathers. Pastor Spight was the childhood friend of a famous preacher, Bishop G.E. Patterson out of Memphis, TN. Pastor introduced me to Bishop Patterson who then introduced me to the world through Christian television networks including TBN, BET and The Word Network. Bishop Patterson gave me the opportunity to preach for him too many times to even count. All of this happened through Pastor Spight, who took me in as a son. I didn't have a father in my life but I saw God cause the Scripture to come to pass that says, "When your mother and father forsake you the Lord will give you mothers and fathers," and such is the case for me. He didn't just give me one either, he gave me mothers and fathers, plural. I don't believe anyone is a self-made man, but I do believe God raises up leaders to father and mother the next generation and open doors for their sons and daughters in the faith. This has become a missing piece in many churches and moves of God, however I believe it will be restored in the church. The Bible says in Malachi,

"Behold, I will send you Elijah the prophet before the coming of the great and dreadful day of the LORD: And he shall turn the heart of the fathers to the children, and the heart of the children to their fathers, lest I come and smite the earth with a curse." Malachi 4:5-6

As I continued to seek the Lord while in Buffalo, I knew God was calling me to begin a ministry and reach people and families for the kingdom. I talked to Pastor Spight about it and received his blessing to start a new work in Buffalo.

In 1993 I started Zion Dominion Global Ministries, a local church with a regional calling to impact lives. Zion Dominion began by renting a banquet room out of the back of a church in downtown Buffalo. Located right on 360 Genesee Street, we quickly outgrew the room and had to move to the YMCA on William and Emslie. Renting the "Y" meant we had to go there every Saturday night to clean off the bingo cards and the beer cans and get it ready for church on Sunday. We got up early and drove the bass and speakers in my truck over to the Y to set up for Sunday service. Our church became a place where families could come and be ministered to. Growing up in a broken family gave me a burden for the whole family, to see God do a work in men, women, and children for His name's sake, what a paradox!

Our church ended up buying the church at 360 Genesee Street, the very place that we previously rented the back banquet room from. It was a true 360 degree return to our roots as a church and a great cause of celebration. I couldn't help but be in awe of what God was building.

We actually put the pastor of the church on a small salary. It was an old church but I saw potential in it. It was located in downtown Buffalo. Some of my friends said it was a raggedy old building, and encouraged me to tear it down and rebuild something. I ended up bringing in a structural engineer to take a look at it. He told me it was structurally strong, just not aesthetically pleasing. I said that's what we are into, rebuilding. Rebuilding people! Even if some don't look like much on the outside, we'll take them. Even if some are messy, we'll take them. Even if some have a lot of baggage they're carrying, a lot of hurts they have walked through, a lot of pain, problems, and mistakes, we'll take them. The structure is still there. The image of God is still there inside every person. It may need to be healed up a bit. It may need to be uncovered, washed, and cleaned up. Just like our building on 360 Genessee, as long as it was structurally sound, we could work with it. So we made the investment and rebuilt the church into a beautiful place to worship and a place where families could come and be made whole by Jesus Christ. Just as we did with that building, we do the same with people. We'll make the investment and build lives and families to impact the world! That church was a prophetic picture of what God was doing in our church. He was changing lives in an unchanging world! 360 degrees, a complete turnaround and it was happening at 360 Genesee Street in Buffalo!

The Lord had spoken to us about the name, *Zion Dominion*. It was a theme that came up time and time again in our ministry and it's a theme we attempt to impart and equip our members with. It was and is my heart's desire to see God prevail in every heart, in every family, in every community for His glory. It is our desire that the people of God be the head and not the tail, at the top and not the bottom, above and not beneath. My desire is to see men and women win at life through the power of the cross. Jesus' work on the cross and victory over death is the greatest source of joy for our lives. Even when circumstances are not going our way, we have the Source of Eternal Joy, Strength, Love, Hope, and Victory. I believe what Jesus taught that the kingdom works as leaven, working its way through the whole dough so that everything in our society is impacted by the gospel. Thusly Zion, the place of God's glory and habitation, would have dominion over all the works of darkness!

The Scripture says, "When Zion travailed she brought forth, before her pain came, she was delivered of a man child." Dominion is a personal conviction for me, the people of God are to come in and take over. We are to use our influence for the betterment of our communities and to serve and reach people for Christ. Anytime you have something that is dominating you are influencing and affecting people. The Scripture calls us the salt of the earth. You can put salt in anything and you can still taste it. Salt also preserves and it purifies. That's what we are about, and that is how the name Zion Dominion manifested. It was destiny for us.

Let's pray.

Father, thank you for the journey you've led us all on. I pray my story would be inspirational to others on their journey and that through your faithfulness to me, others would be inspired and called to serve you likewise. In Jesus' powerful and awesome name. Amen.

3 WALKING IT OUT

One of my personal burdens is family. Because I grew up in a broken family and a slightly dysfunctional one at that, my personal prayer became, "God let me be the father to my children that I never had and let me be the husband to my wife that my mother never saw." Because of this burden and what God worked in my heart, the focus of our church has been on covenant. The first family in the Bible was dysfunctional, so it's no surprise that many families today are operating in disfunction.

The truth is God is the Creator of family and the Maker of covenant. Before there ever was a church, there was the family. When the family became dysfunctional, he established the church. And even when He did, in the New Testament He called it the household of faith.

As we have therefore opportunity, let us do good unto all men, especially unto them who are of the household of faith. Galatians 6:10

Family is on God's mind. It is His design and it is my heart to see God's purpose, design, and destiny for every family be reached in our church, community, and region. As a church we are focused on reaching men for Christ. I believe as the man goes, so goes the family. So our focus has been on the man. Our church is somewhat of an anomaly with 45% of our members male. That's about double the national average, which I am happy about, but there is more work to be done. I know that if you can get the man, you can get the whole family for the kingdom. It's a hard task, it's a daunting task. Most churches average about 20-25% male. I don't say this to boast, but to challenge us to go further and pray harder for men!

People see that there is a propensity for women to be more avid church attendees than men, but I have always believed in general the church doesn't really preach a message that appeals to the man's psyche. We've generally made church more accommodating to women, more service opportunities for women, more programs for women to connect. We have Bible studies at times that make sense for women. Many churches provide childcare for the women to connect, but the men are left without a time to meet, to connect, and to grow in their faith. Now don't get me wrong, we are all about reaching women at Zion Dominion, but not to the neglect of the man. We have many programs for women. My wife Pamela is very involved in reaching out to young women and developing ministries to meet their needs, but we saw the need for the whole family to be a part of our community. We started being more intentional and deliberate about speaking to and addressing men in our services and we started to get a change. Our focus has been on family and the infrastructure of the family. We've focused on the man's responsibility as priest to his home and women's response as his helpmete. Now I don't mean some archaic, outdated approach, but a biblical approach. The biblical design for a family is what we see in Scripture and it's what we have endeavored to live, teach, and impart into people. It's one of the reasons we have been able to grow from 20 people in 1993 to over 4,000 people currently. I don't say that condescendingly, I want to share what has worked for us. What God did in my life in giving me mothers and fathers, and the support of a Christian family of faith, I knew he wanted to do in the life of our congregation. I wanted to see this replicated and multiplied in and through our church. I sought to build mentoring relationships with the older men and the younger men. The older women and the younger women. This is how the kingdom grows and expands, through relationships, and through mothers and fathers investing in others. There are Esthers as well as Ruths and Naomies to mentor women to become the women of God they are destined to be. Our goal is to have fathers and mothers in the faith to nurture and encourage one another and grow into the fullness of what God has for us as a community of grace and faith. For the women it comes down to building multigenerational discipleship making opportunities as Paul wrote in Titus,

"The aged women likewise, that *they be* in behaviour as becometh holiness, not false accusers, not given to much wine, teachers of good things; That they may teach the young women to be sober, to love their husbands, to love their children, *To be* discreet, chaste, keepers at home, good, obedient to their own husbands, that the word of God be not blasphemed." Titus 2:3-5

"For though ye have ten thousand instructors in Christ, yet *have ye* not many fathers: for in Christ Jesus I have begotten you through the gospel." I Corinthians 4:15

In terms of reaching people, my perspective is we're preaching the gospel with a concept called indiscriminate dissipation. Where you turn on a water hose and whatever bottle gets filled is filled. So there really is no targeted audience, but as we began to preach in a way to reach both the men and the women, we started to see some real results. Many times in the black church the Peretto Law is so pervasive, 80% female,

22

20% male, is what the demographic breakdown looks like. There is a propensity to preach the sensual side of Christ - in the sense that He is bread when you're hungry, water when you're thirsty, roof over your head, clothes on your back. The problem is many of those things men want to be to their families, to provide these things so that doesn't appeal to the psyche of men. To address this more fully, I went back and reassessed the Scriptures to see how God dealt with the disciples. I found that He dealt with the disciples differently than He did with the women of the Scriptures. When He dealt with the men He gave them directions and commands. That's how a man really functions. You ask a man his name, he'll tell you what his name is, the next question we ask is, "What do you do?" Men measure themselves by their productivity, so if a man is unproductive, he feels he has no worth. So anytime you can tap into the spirit of a man and ignite purpose, you've got a productive citizen. The problem is if people are just coming to church through perfunctory attendance and have no real zeal, no real drive to be stimulated by the gospel or the fellowship of the saints, he is just going to eventually start dropping his wife and children off and picking them up after the service. My target then began to focus on speaking to the man in particular and that's how I came up with the biblical concepts you need to live and to lead. Those have really been the truths that have changed the direction of our ministry. The man is not the head of the house, he is the head of the wife. Westernized culture and theology has presupposed that man is the head of the house but he is really the head of the wife. According to Corinthians the head of every woman is man, the head of every man is Christ, the head of Christ is God.

But I would have you know, that the head of every man is Christ; and the head of the woman is the man; and the head of Christ is God. 1 Corinthians 11:3

So we began celebrating every man, even if the husband is unsaved. In that case you've just got an unsaved head. If he's not that productive, you've got an unproductive head, but he is the head by default not by performance. When you start empowering the man from that perspective, it changes the game. Men feel empowered by God's grace to become who they are in Christ. They begin living in the identity of who they are and who they are meant to be. Empowering people to be and do what God has said and invited them to, changes everything! We now have a community of activated people functioning in the finished work of Calvary and teaching others to do the same. This changes the game!

As we've made strides in this area to deliver the gospel in a way that reaches the whole family, I realized that our approach and many churches' approach had become overly emotional. You have to have pragmatism with your spirituality. Men need direction and directives, that is what men respond to. Men want to be challenged and given directions and commands. Men are hard wired this way by God. Instruct a man in what to do and he'll do it. Simple as that. He'll do it well and he'll take pride in what he did and feel accomplished in his work. Same thing with the things of God. Make it clear to the man what they need to do so they can go out and do it. Then they'll be fired up when they come to church next week, telling their friends how they did and challenging one another to do it all over again. Men bond over this kind of thing. They connect over activity and action. So we give the men a challenge and an assignment. Men are about putting their faith into action. They aren't as apt to sit around and talk about their faith as women might or call each other to discuss a relationship problem. Men want action and if our preaching can direct them into action with commands and directives, I am speaking their language. They're not going to come back empty handed. In some churches though, a woman hears the message and then goes home and tells her husband and friends how great the preacher preached, as if to try to get the man to come hear him. That doesn't work!

The man at home is not being celebrated like that, so some men will have a subconscious chip on their shoulder before they even get to church, because the preacher is being celebrated, and he's just being tolerated. Ladies, that's not how to motivate your husband or boyfriend to participate in church. At Zion Dominion we have women who have unsaved husbands. I tell them just say what the Lord has done, don't say anything about me. Because to another man, I am just competition for attention. Through ignorance you can make men a needless casualty of our war. Instead of coming to church to be completed, they feel they are there in competition. It has to be a focused approach and intentional. Our church is 45% male not by accident or serendipity. We targeted men!

Proverbs tells us, "A wise woman builds her house, but a foolish woman tears hers down with her own hands."

Joshua said, "As for me and my house, we will serve the Lord." Joshua here is talking about his family, not his house, the building. There is a big difference. We teach women to testify and give honor to God and to her husband who is the head of her life. If a man hears that, no matter where he is standing, it gives him some worth, it's not slight of hand, it's legitimate.

And so we have endeavored to make this teaching on the role of the man a intricate part of our culture. We've seen God do great things in families when the man and the woman take their rightful place in God's design, families work.

Likewise, ye wives, *be* in subjection to your own husbands; that, if any obey not the word, they also may without the word be won by the conversation of the wives; 1 Peter 3:1

Let's pray.

Father thank you for family. Thank you for the burden you've given us to see families healed, restored, and to become all you created them to be. Lord we pray for the men of our communities to come to you. We pray they would rise up and be the leaders you've called them to be. I pray for the wives that they would come to you, hear from you, know your word and influence their families toward a relationship with you. We thank you for the family, now let your will be done, let your kingdom come here on earth as it is in heaven. In Jesus' name. Amen.

4 WHO YOU WALK WITH IS WHO YOU TALK WITH

Once we begin reaching the family, my passion is for discipleship and raising people and champions for Christ. The reality is if you embrace the biblical concept of holiness, it impacts every area of your life. Holiness is a lifestyle. It affects how you live, how you handle money, how you treat your spouse. Look at St. Mark Chapter 10,

46 And they came to Jericho: and as he went out of Jericho with his disciples and a great number of people, blind Bartimaeus, the son of Timaeus, sat by the highway side begging. 47 And when he heard that it was Jesus of Nazareth, he began to cry out, and say, Jesus, thou son of David, have mercy on me. 48 And many charged him that he should hold his peace: but he cried the more a great deal, Thou son of David, have mercy on me. 49 And Jesus stood still, and commanded him to be called. And they call the blind man, saying unto him, Be of good comfort, rise; he calleth thee. 50 And he, casting away his garment, rose, and came to Jesus. 51 And Jesus answered and said unto him, What wilt thou that I should do unto thee? The blind man said unto him, Lord, that I might receive my sight. 52 And Jesus said unto him, Go thy way; thy faith hath made thee whole. And immediately he

received his sight, and followed Jesus in the way.

The truth is who you walk with is who you talk with. Who walks with thee is who talks with thee. In this passage of Scripture, Bartimeus is running into Jesus, if you will, while Jesus is coming out of Jericho. Someone took Bartimaeus there and dropped him off to beg. He's blind and the Scripture says when he heard that Jesus was near, he began to cry out, "Son of David, have mercy on me." He didn't live here but he was desperate for God. Bartimaeus calling Jesus, "Son of David" means he acknowledged by faith that Jesus is the King. You can't call Him, "the man upstairs," you can't call Him your "buddy." You can't call Him something He is not. Bartimaeus said, "Son of David, have mercy on me." You want to have the kind of praise that will cause Jesus to stop in his tracks and give you his undivided attention.

When Bartimaeus calls Jesus, he doesn't know where He is, he is just calling out everywhere. He knew He was close because they are telling him to be quiet. Anytime someone tells you to be quiet, you've got to know you're getting close. Close to your breakthrough! Close to your answered prayer! Close to the Father's will for your life!

In Mark, Jesus responds to Bartimaeus and calls him by name. Sometimes you've got to speak up and tell God what you need. Not that He needs to know but for your own sake, you've got to speak up. You need to have people in your life who know how to speak up. Not that He doesn't know what you have need of before you ask or think, but you've got to tell God you are in agreement with what He wants to do in your life. So they told him to be quiet and he called out all the more. When you express your agreement with what God wants to do and speak it out loud, it has power to release faith for the answer.

Koinonia is the Greek word for fellowship. Sometimes you don't walk with people because of pride. You've got to be humble enough and vulnerable enough to allow people to speak into your life, so that God can move in your life. If I've got the wrong people walking with me, I will miss out. I don't need to know that you know how I feel. I need you to tell me what God says; I can't have that if I don't have right communion. People are coming to church without fellowship and communication with others. We need to walk with people who talk with you and know you and can speak into your life and help you see and know what God is doing. Who you walk with and who you talk with make a big difference. You need to take advice from people who know God, hear God, and agree with God. That's why you need the right people around you to know what God says, who challenge you with the word of God!

Where are the Christians who will come to the altar to call upon the Lord and wait on Him? You need people around you agreeing with God's will for your life, not their will. Not their ideas, not man made solutions, but God's plan and will.

For some people church has become a drive through, a McDonald's. They come and they go. But you need to have people you are walking with. Check your connections. I need people who speak into my life and get me convicted, to get me on track. They love me enough to talk to me. The reason we don't do that is we don't have communion. How are you going to walk with me unless you talk with me? We learn a valuable lesson from Bartimaeus.

Somewhere in his walk, Bartimaeus changes who he is walking with. He is only speaking for himself here, crying out to Jesus for help. He receives his sight and then he follows Jesus. When Jesus speaks into your life, there is no substitution for His word. Troubles don't last always, He is going to turn this around. When Jesus said, "I am the way," He was clear no one else was leading, He was the leader. They were His disciples. They followed Him. He was in charge and they were learning as apprentices.

Why are you going after people who don't want to walk with you? I don't go after people who don't want me. You can't force people to walk with you. But what you can do is walk with God, allow Him to speak into your situation, show you how to deal with this, and get over this and follow Him.

I don't know if you've ever read the story about the Feral children. They were raised by dogs. Their parents were killed on a hunting trip by coyotes. The children were babies and survived the attack, the animals didn't kill them. The dogs, instead of killing the babies, raised them. The children were found 10 years later, on four legs, with callouses two inches thick on the back of their hands. Because who you walk with is who you talk with. They couldn't say anything, couldn't articulate anything. People thought they were mentally handicap, but they weren't. It's just they were walking with dogs, so they were acting like dogs. Simple as that. It took another ten years to get them back on track. They had to put boards on their knees to keep them on their feet. But as they changed their situation and who they were being influenced by, they changed their lives. Who they walked with was who they talked with, and as a result they acted like them.

You need to walk with people who believe in victory. Hang out with people who God has done something for and you'll start believing God can do it for you. I want to walk with people who have experienced victory and healing. Don't ONLY talk about how sick you are, but how victorious God is. I want to hear your testimony on what the word of God says for your situation, because He is the Lord who healeth me. This is about changing the conversation. We need to have a testimony of what God does, according to Ephesians 3:20.

"Now unto him that is able to do exceeding abundantly above all that we ask or think, according to the power that worketh in us."

Say something victorious. Claim something victorious. You can make it. God is a healer. God is going to turn this around. As presiding Bishop Charles E. Blake says, "I see you in your future and you look much better than you do right now!" Good things are coming your way.

The Scripture says Bartimaeus followed Jesus. People these days almost need to be bribed to come to church because people haven't had a real metamorphosis. They haven't really been changed. Thank Him for the already! It's already done. You're already healed. You're already blessed! Thank Him for the already. Not getting ready. You're standing in the already! Find someone who will talk to you and tell you, you're in the already. You're already saved and healed. The child is already following God. I know how you feel, because I am in my already too! Somewhere in your walk with God you've got to get around people who have some power. Holy Ghost power! Who can speak prophetically into your life. If the Bible isn't what it says, then this wouldn't work. But it is the truth!

Will a lion roar in the forest, when he hath no prey? Will a young lion cry out of his den, if he have taken nothing? The prophet Amos says everything has a cause and an effect.

How can you walk together unless you are agreed? Amos 3:3-4

.If you don't have any vulnerability, you won't have any victory. You've got to make yourself vulnerable, that's how you get victory. I have no problem asking people to pray for me. I need prayer. I ask people to come into agreement with me. I need prayer especially since I am a pastor. I don't walk around like I have everything all together. Being open and honest is what it means to have communion and fellowship. God can have someone around you that may not have all the answers, but they've got an answer for your situation. Who you walk with is who you talk with. You need strong brothers and sisters to walk and talk with. If the people you walk with talk defeat, failure, and hurt, you're going to be walking in that. Walking in defeat. But I see a better future for you already. If you said to me, "Pray for me because I am going through this or that," I'll tell you I already see you out. I see *already* on you. You're already healed. You're already free. You're already there!

I don't see blind Bartimaeus telling the others, "Hey guys." No, the Bible says he followed Jesus. He came out of his garments. What does that have to do with following Jesus? They gave him begging clothes so he could look pitiful, but when your eyes are opened and Jesus calls you, you'll take off that pitiful stuff. Think about this, how does he take off his garments that he hasn't seen? When you can't see, your other senses are acute! When Jesus told him to come, he said, I can't even see it, but I am coming out of it! You need to come out of it even before you see it. Those were his clothes but he came out of them! You can hear better and you can smell better. It's like he said, "I know what I have on and it's filthy and it's smelly. So when Jesus calls me, I am coming out of this before I even come to him." That was blind

Bartimaeus, but he isn't blind anymore.

How are you going to walk with the Son of David, the King, if you have pauper clothes on? You've got to come out of it, because you're walking with the King. He's talking kingdom, dominion, and authority. You're walking with Christ now. When you start coming out of bondage, nothing is going to hinder you from giving God your best praise. Who you walk with is who you talk with!

Nothing is going to hinder me from giving you glory, from giving you my best praise. You're coming out of your situation and nothing is going to inhibit you from giving God glory.

Let's pray.

Father, I thank you that who I walk with is who I talk with. Lord, I thank you that relationships matter, that people matter, and that you have called me to be an influence on others, to be a blessing to others, to reveal you to others. Help me to recognize your leading, follow your guidance and become like you in my actions so that you get all the glory. In Jesus' name I pray. Amen.

5 THIS IS FOR PRAISERS ONLY

Even of the covenant which he made with Abraham, and of his oath unto Isaac; And hath confirmed the same to Jacob for a law, and to Israel for an everlasting covenant, Saying, Unto thee will I give the land of Canaan, the lot of your inheritance; When ye were but few, even a few, and strangers in it. And when they went from nation to nation, and from one kingdom to another people; He suffered no man to do them wrong: yea, he reproved kings for their sakes, Saying, Touch not mine anointed, and do my prophets no harm. 1 Chronicles 16:19

Caution, this is for praises only. When David moved the ark 7 spaces in chapter 15 and no one died, it's coming off the heals of Uzzah touching the cart, moving the ark of the covenant, and dying.

David was married to a non-praiser. You can still be in the church with those who aren't praisers. As a result of David praising God and his wife not being a praiser, she began to call him a fool. David told her she hadn't seen anything yet. David was just getting started in his praising. He was about to get even more undignified than this! David praised until his clothes fell off which is metaphorical for your and my situation. You've got to praise until you come out of whatever you're in!

When David came out front he smelled like the sheep, because whatever God has called you to do, you ought to smell like it. You ought to be so immersed in the calling that God has for you that you actually start smelling like it. You shouldn't smell like weed, alcohol, or the club. God has called you to smell like what he's called you to. You should smell like victory, worship, joy, myrrh, and frankincense. You shouldn't smell like the world when you come to church on Sunday, that smell will deceive you.

David picks praisers from the praise team. Yes, you ought to be a praiser. Psalm 150 tells us that everything that has breath should praise the Lord. You were made for praise, for the high praise of God. You were designed for more. You were made to experience God in praise. Nothing in this world will satisfy like God will through praise. You were made to worship, and if you're not worshipping God, you're worshipping something!

In chapter 16 though, David is about to go into the land of Canaan but only a few of the men could come with him. He needed to choose the men. You need some people with you who can flow with you on the journey. You're going to face surprises, adventures, and challenges along the way. You need some professional praisers for the trip. No offense to anyone, but not everyone can go with you where you are going because you don't even know where you are going. God has set up your future wonderfully, but you can't see it. If you could see where you are going and how good it's going to be, your joy would be so full. I am going to give you a peek into what God has in store in this chapter, so get ready, your joy is about to go up to another level!

Just because things don't look right, doesn't mean you're looking right at what doesn't look right. Some things don't look right now, because you are not where you are supposed to be. Let me explain...

There is a story of a blind man in the Bible who all he could see was trees. Jesus told him to take another look. As far as his vision was concerned, things weren't looking right. So he took another look and they looked like men. Sometimes you need to take another look because you're not close enough to what God wants you to see because you haven't moved yet. Sometimes you need to take that first step, to start moving, and then take another look.

David picked a handful of people to go with him. He couldn't bring everyone, he needed to narrow down his list and take only a select few. So he decided to take Asaph, the chief Levite, the lead singer. Asaph would sing when no one else wanted to. When there is no atmosphere, when there is no mic, when you don't have a song of your own, you need an Asaph. You need someone who will lift your vision, ignite your praise, lift you up when you are down. I know for me, if I am feeling low, I need to find someone who is up when I am down. When I need an answer, when I need my medical results, I need someone who is going to praise with me through the storm.

Jehiel was another person David choose. He was a gatekeeper. While you are trying to do what God has called you to do, Jehiels protect you, they don't allow you to hear crazy stuff. They watch out for you and they help you.

Benaiah was a bodyguard, another person who David took with him. He's another worshipper and he's a bodyguard. Benaiah is the type who watches over you, while you are trying to do what God has called you to do. You need someone like this, who won't let demons and devils mess up your flow. He's a worshipper and a body guard.

Jehallelel   is a warrior, a Levite. This group has a whole new assignment. They are for you, where you are getting ready to go. That's the difference between a warrior and a buddy! I need a praiser on my side who will go out before my destiny, and help me through anything trying to mess up my future!

David choose men skilled in what they do and men with an attitude of praise. Men who would praise through the storm and stand with him through the trials.

Are you a praiser?

The people David took with him were all praisers. I want to suggest this was a game changer for David and can be for you and I as well. There are some of God's promises that are accessed only by praise. Only by persistent, steadfast, immovable praise. Praise that doesn't stop or get offended. Praise that rises higher than our circumstances. Praise that comes from devoting time to the secret place, between you and God. When you know God in the secret place, you'll be able to help others. It's not until you find God for yourself, that you can minister to the needs of others.

So I want to ask you again, are you a praiser? Or are you a complainer?

Do you let the circumstances of life sway you or do you stand firm in what the Lord has called you to? These people don't quit because they got laid off, or got a flat tire. They get there because they know they have an assignment. They are not here to entertain, they sing through the storm, through the cold, through the fever. I am talking about people who don't quit when the circumstances are difficult, but who remain with you in the good times and the bad times! I am not talking about fair weather friends, I am talking about the faithful, who remain full of praise when life throws a curveball!

Record, thank, and praise God. Or in the original text: invoke, record, and praise God. This is what you are - praisers from another dimension. To invoke is to summon. To invoke God you call Him and He hears you. All the Levites couldn't do that. See, if you start singing a song and did not invoke the Lord, God's not here, you're just wasting time. If I am on my journey I need to be praising God in the dark, and when I start singing my song, God is here, whether you show up or not, God is here. To record means to be with you on the journey and write some things down. Write down what God has showed you or find someone who will, so you can remember what the Lord has done for you.

"Now go, write it before them in a table, and note it in a book, that it may be for the time to come for ever and ever." Isaiah 30:8

That time when you almost got in the car crash and you called on the Name of Jesus and He delivered you. Write it down! You need someone with you who will help you remember God's deliverance. That's why you can't get happy. You are all alone. There is no one who can come and not thank God for what He has done. We remember what God has done and we talk about it every week. This is how we overcome, by the word of our testimony.

"And they overcame him by the blood of the Lamb, and by the word of their testimony; and they loved not their lives unto the death." Revelation 12:11

Praisers won't let you pout. I know they don't like you, but I know God likes you. I know what they did, but I know what God said. You need some people who are praisers around you, those who won't let you stay down. Ask your friends who are they to you. Who are you to your friends? Are you letting your friends sulk in their pain and disappointment, or do you call them out with praise?

I don't just want buddies, I want praisers only. Possessing the promised land is for praisers only. Those who won't let you stay stuck in your defeat but who will encourage you to come out of it.

You see when you are surrounded by the right praisers and the right people, others can do God's prophets no harm because they have the right people in place. This is for you today if you are in a strange place. It's strange because you've never seen this before. You're going to be strangers here, but this is what God has for you. You can't be apprehensive of new heights when you have the right people around you to understand the immensity of the Lord's presence!

You've seen the parent who isn't happy with their kids just dragging them along. Some of you have been where others are trying to go and you need to be gentle. It is a strange place because you're used to where you are however, in order to go to new heights and new dimensions you need to lead out with praise. Some of you may be changing directions or careers, in your personal lives, you may not know how you are going to make it. God gives you Levites who write things down and remind you of the things God has done for you, for them and for others. You need people like this.

If you're married to a praiser, they're thanking God for the food and saying longer prayers than usual. They thank God for everything. When they're driving, when they're cleaning, when they're on the phone, when they're alone in the yard. When you're married to a praiser, they are giving God praise all the time. They praise God for baby steps and for everything. And if you're smart, if you don't know anyone like that, find a new place in your church and get around people who start praising. Sit in the middle of them, because praisers smell like praise. When you get close enough, it will get all over you and you'll start praising and loving God just like them also! Praising God is contagious. Once you get a taste of it, you won't be able to stop. The Bible tells us to taste and see that the Lord is good!

"O taste and see that the LORD is good: blessed is the man that trusteth in him." Psalm 34:8

Sometimes praise sounds like a banshee or a scream. So release the sound of praise and your praise will fight for you. Get around others who will join you in praise. The Bible says when they were together, there was a suddenly that happened. A sound like a rushing wind!

"And suddenly there came a sound from heaven as of a rushing mighty wind, and it filled all the house where they were sitting." Acts 2:2

Sound can not come from a place unless it goes to a place. You can't hear me if I can't hear you. Sound can't go to a place unless it comes from a place. So when you give God praise, your sound goes to a place. A sound like a rushing wind came from a place and filled the place where they were. I don't know what you might need right now, but anyone who has a deficit, God can fill it. So get your praise on and things are going to start leaving your finances, your health, your family and God is going to fill that place when you begin to praise. Fill what is lacking with praise. Praisers thank God for everything! Not just on Sundays. They make praise a lifestyle and they rise above their circumstances. Take that step of faith and obedience, and allow God to work not only in your circumstances, but most importantly in your heart, making you more like Him.

Let's pray.

Father, I thank you that you've given us the ability to praise. Thank you that I was made to praise. Thank you that you inhabit our praise. You fill us with your joy and enable us to stand upon the heights with you when we choose to praise. No matter what it looks like or feels like, I am going to choose to praise you in this storm. I believe I will see your goodness in the land of the living.

6 THE DIARY OF A DOUBLE BLESSING

And as he entered into a certain village, there met Him ten men that were lepers, which stood afar off: And they lifted up their voices and said Jesus, Master, have mercy on us. And when He saw them, He said unto them, go shew yourselves unto the priests. And it came to pass, that as they went, they were cleansed. And one of them, when he saw that he was healed, turned back, and with a loud voice glorified God, and fell down on his face at his feet, giving him thanks: and he was a Samaritan. And Jesus answering said, Were there not ten cleansed? Where are the nine? There are not found that returned to give glory to God, save this stranger. And He said unto him, Arise, go thy way: thy faith hath made thee whole. And when he was demanded of the Pharisees, when the kingdom of God should come, he answered them and said, The kingdom of God cometh not with observation: Neither shall they say, Lo here! or, lo there! for, behold, the kingdom of God is within you. Luke 17:11-21

Rhema is a greek word meaning right now. If you've been asking God for something, I believe God is going to release a double portion of whatever you've been asking him for. Somebody's believing God for this, He says, "I've got that too! Double!" Somebody's believing God to make a way, He's going to make two ways. Somebody's believing God to open a door, He's going to open two doors!

You may be saying, "I know I am not supposed to be here," but you've waited long enough, you've got a double portion coming.

For your shame ye shall have double; and for confusion they shall rejoice in their portion: therefore in their land they shall possess the double: everlasting joy shall be unto them. Isaiah 61:7

He's the God of more than enough!
The God of abundance!
The God of increase!

Lepers were a far way off and the law said they couldn't come close to the rest of society. They were outcasts, no one could touch them and they couldn't touch anyone, less the disease be transmitted to other victims. The sores were a terrible sight to see. People hid from the lepers and the lepers hid from the people. But they did have each other and together 10 of them made their way toward Jesus. This in itself was a huge step of faith! And we see Jesus didn't just heal one of them, he healed them all.

What you've been believing God for, God said I will double it. I love that it's in the text. 10 lepers came and saw Jesus afar off. Levitical law said because you are full of leprosy you can't get close. They've written you off, ostracized you. But instead of stopping there, they kept looking, kept hoping. The Scripture says, they saw him afar off. All you need to do is see Him, if I can just get in his face, if I could just see Him, and they said, "Jesus have mercy on us!" Jesus told them, "Go show yourself to the priest." He had just performed a miracle responding to their step of faith in coming to Him alone for their healing. Jesus told them to show yourself to the priest, as they went they were cleansed. I am convinced you can't get cleansed when there is no one we can show ourselves to! The problem is we've got dirty people and because of it we can't show ourselves to anyone. But as they went, they were cleansed. When you show yourself to dirty people, they can't pronounce you clean. I don't want to judge, I don't want to indict anyone, however if you don't have anyone to show yourself to, you can't be cleansed! This is the secret struggle of many people. They are struggling with weaknesses or sin, but they don't have anyone they can trust to pray with them, to walk with them, to talk with them, and the struggle rages within. But if you would reach out today and show yourself, open up to another believer, I believe you would begin to experience a new level of freedom, a new level of victory in your life.

The truth is homosexuality is wrong.
Transgenderism is wrong.

Lesbianism is wrong.

Adultery is wrong.

Whoredom is wrong.

Fornication is wrong.

They are not spirits, but works of the flesh!

Galatians 5 explains this fact!

If you don't have anyone in your life to show yourself to, you may be in trouble.

You need someone to show yourself to so they can tell you it's unclean, but then they help clean you. They help you out of the struggle you're in, so you can live in the freedom God intended for you.

You gotta make a judgement. Jesus told him, "Go show yourself to the priest." This is for all the people who say, I just need Jesus. You need people in your life also! They went to the priests and the priests declared they were cleansed. As they went they were cleansed. There is a state of being called ataraxia, a state of freedom from emotional disturbance, freedom from psychological disturbance. I believe that is what God wants for us today. What's worrying you today? God wants to free you from it!

If I can show myself to someone and they can declare for me what I can't declare for myself, that I am free, that I have favor on my life, you're going to experience the freedom the lepers experienced. Then you will go back and tell God, "thank you." If you are believing God for this, begin to thank Him. Not one of the lepers came back except this stranger, this alien, this Samaritan. May I submit to you that the 9 couldn't come back if they tried. The one couldn't stay away if he tried. What is one out of 10? That's the tithe, the tithe belongs to God, so when He blesses you, go back and thank God. So when He turns it, come back and get the double blessing. The Bible says they were cleansed, purged of their illness and diseases, but the one when he realized what happened went back to say thanks. If you read the text, they never got close enough to Jesus. They weren't allowed to get close to the priest. So now that he was cleansed he could get close. He came back, he gave Him praise, and Jesus said that faith has made you whole. You were already cleansed, but now you are whole.

If you had leprosy they had to burn your clothes, everything you touch is unclean. So Jesus healing them of leprosy, forever changed their lives, their relationships, and their status in the community. They would never be the same again. So he came back to give Him thanks. The disease has stopped so he came back to say thanks. As he does, He starts restoring every part of the leper's life. When God is done with you, people will not comprehend what you've been through, because God is making you whole!

Joseph was sold into prison and left for dead. When they came back they didn't even recognize him. They meant it for evil, but God meant it for good. God took the evil Joseph's brothers did and He used it to transform Joseph's life. He was unrecognizable because of the transformation. What are you believing God for today that needs a transformation? What needs to change? What needs a touch from God in your life? Show yourself to Him today.

Anytime God puts favor on you, it doesn't fit! You don't deserve to get it, it's favor for your future. My children's pastors were pregnant with their 3rd child. They were in the middle of building a house, working as an executive in management and he got laid off. His job was eliminated. You don't get two week notices at the management level and on top of that they were trying to build a house. Questions were racing. How would they finish it? What would they do? The truth of the matter is our God is able. Whatever you are believing God for, He's going to double it. So my children's pastor comes in my office and shows me the picture of the house he built. They finished it after losing his job! They were about to move in and he got double the garage and double the size! So he lost his job, but he got double the blessing! God is not limited by your employment status. He is God no matter where you are or what situation you find yourself in!

What are you believing God for? There is a double portion for you. God confirms His word with signs following.

Joseph was a governor with a new coat in Egypt. He got married. He had a son, and named him Manasseh, which means he makes me forget!

One year we had a terrible storm as I was going to church. I shoveled the sidewalk before I left. I had messed up my back. So after shoveling before I left for vacation, my back started killing me, hurting bad. I asked someone else to lead the prayer meeting because it was paining me badly. My wife came in and started massaging my back. She gets on a prayer call and begins praying for me, she is laying her hands on my back. She's got her head on my back, speaking in tongues, and then she says there it is, meaning my healing. She believed something broke during her prayer. However, my back was still killing me. I got to the service and the Holy Spirit said again, "She said there it is." So I started running around and my back was healed! All the pain left! God blessed me with a Manasseh blessing! He made me forget that my back was hurt. He made me forget because He blessed me so!

You got to find someone you can show yourself to! I showed myself to my wife and I got what I was believing for. I needed that. I got double! They never got to Jesus, sometimes you just need Him to say something to you! He said your faith has made you *sozo* - whole. Freedom from emotional disturbance. Tranquility and no emotional anxiety. He will keep you in perfect peace, whose mind is stayed on thee. Beware of the day when churches stop having altar calls! I have preached in many places that have no altar. No place to come and encounter God. Churches with 5,000-10,000 seats, but no altar!

If your blessing could talk, it would tell you to go back and give thanks! I have known many people when they are in crisis, they're tearing the church doors down. Now that everything is good they don't come around anymore. You need to come back and give thanks. Whatever you ask Him for, today is a day of the double!

Then Joseph has another son, his name is Ephraim, which means doubly blessed, multiplied, fruitful. It was enough that you made me forget, then you're going to bless me double! Thank you Jesus! Whatever it is, I have no room for it because I am full of my Manasseh blessing and the Ephraim blessing! This is the diary of the double blessing. It says whatever God has done, come back and tell Him thank you. Get your second wind and give Him more thanks for the double!

Let's pray.

Father we thank you for the double blessing. Thank you for your provision in our lives, and the way you care for your children. Thank you that you are the Father we never had, and the perfect Savior who gave yourself for our sins. Thank you for the breath we breathe so that we can give you praise and experience the abundant life you have given us. We thank you for it in Jesus' name. Amen.

7 AN ENEMY HAS DONE THIS

24 Another parable put he forth unto them, saying, The kingdom of heaven is likened unto a man which sowed good seed in his field: 25 But while men slept, his enemy came and sowed tares among the

wheat, and went his way. 26 But when the blade was sprung up, and brought forth fruit, then appeared the tares also. 27 So the servants of the householder came and said unto him, Sir, didst not thou sow good seed in thy field? from whence then hath it tares? 28 He said unto them, An enemy hath done this. The servants said unto him, Wilt thou then that we go and gather them up? 29 But he said, Nay; lest while ye gather up the tares, ye root up also the wheat with them. 30 Let both grow together until the harvest: and in the time of harvest I will say to the reapers, Gather ye together first the tares, and bind them in bundles to burn them: but gather the wheat into my barn. Matthew 13:24-30

63 The fire consumed their young men; and their maidens were not given to marriage. 64 Their priests fell by the sword; and their widows made no lamentation. 65 Then the Lord awaked as one out of sleep, and like a mighty man that shouteth by reason of wine. Psalm 78:63-65

Jesus shifts the parable from the ground being us and the seed being the Word, which He stated earlier in Matthew 13 when He gives the parable about the sower and the seed. He shifts it to where the ground is no longer the focus but it is the seed. The seed becomes you and I. The Scripture says a man had a field and sowed seeds of wheat. While he slept, an enemy came and sowed tare in the field. When things began to grow, they questioned the seed. Jesus' response was to allow the wheat to grow with the tares and in the days of harvest, the two would be separated. What we miss here is once seed has been sown someone has to stay awake and watch over the grounds. Even today, while you are sleeping, being desensitized, the enemy is wreaking havoc over your marriage, children, and home.

Some would argue that the enemy is going to come no matter what. Well, not exactly. The enemy will not come against the saints of God without an opening. The enemy is waiting for you to fall asleep so he can have his way in your life. Once you do, he brings discord and then disappears. He leaves you wondering what happened over night. What I can tell you is an enemy has done this.

Let us look at the significance of the tare, which is often looked at as a weed. One, there is a conflict with the wheat and the seeds. The tares here are darlo weed. It has black venomous seeds and lives not in the soil but off the roots of the wheat. Take it as this, there are people living and growing off you. They need you to sustain life. No matter how much you grow, they are still with you. Before you become upset and ask God to remove them, He is letting you know no matter what you are in or what is on you, you can still grow. The tares did not stop the wheat from growing. It does not matter who is in your life, who is attempting to mess up your future, you will grow. Nothing can stop your germination once God has planted you. He wants you to bloom and have posterity while you have all the poison attached to you. Yet if you do not bloom, it is the gardener's fault. He does not remove the tares in your life -- the bad family and heartache. You grow with the appalling friends, the job you can't stand, or the dysfunctional marriage.

For the people that breakdown quickly and give up easily, you should look at yourself and see if you are what God said you are. If you cannot grow with the burdens of life on your back, you may not be God planted. He said in His Word,

"...In the world you will have tribulation. But take heart; I have overcome the world." John 16:33.

Since He overcame the world, you are able to do it too. Say to yourself, "I'm going to grow in whatever I have to, to reach my full potential in Christ. If my back is against the wall, I will grow. If the bottom drops from underneath me, I will grow." There is nothing in this world to stop you from being what God has called you to be. God is still in control of the ground. No demon in hell, nor force on earth can cancel out the assignment He has called you to. You will not wither away because of your environment. God will provide you enough nutrients to sustain your life and that which threatens to kill you.

Unfortunately, some us will abort our functionally of our maturation by making excuses as to why we can't grow. People say things like, "I have to get out of this town," or "I came from a bad family." Some blame it on a time long removed, "My daddy wasn't around when I was coming up." But through all of this, He wants you to grow. Don't abort your present and future because of your past or what your situation looks like.

In the Scripture, it doesn't say the wheat stopped growing. The Scripture says,

"Gather the weeds first and bind them in bundles to be burned, but gather the wheat into my barn." Matthew 13:30.

The wheat still grew with the poison (people) that feed off its roots. As I read these passages, I realized the wheat needed the tares to grow with it, to grows stronger. You need people in your life to give you resistance as you mature. It helps you to build tenacity as you press forward. This is why the parable instructs us to allow the two to grow together or the wheat shall be destroyed. The problem is people don't know who to blame for their problems.

In these last days, our families have become a target of the enemy. Psalm 78:63-65 says,

"The fire consumed their young men, and their maidens were not given in marriage. Their priests fell by the sword, and their widows made no lamentation."

Allow me to show you how an enemy has done this, yet again. The fire consumed their young men –they are dying before their time. The men are dying in the streets and from the lack of ambition to live. Young men die from the loss of identity by deciding to abandon the natural desires for women. Their maidens were not given in marriage – young women are saying there are no good men. Since the fall of Adam and Eve, a woman's heart desire was that of a man – a husband in particular. Through time, the desires for a husband have seemed to diminish. Women are more comfortable with being the head of the house more than ever. There was a few decades where a husband was needed, but now, he's an option that many are opting out of. Marriage was seen as a form of stability not liability. In most cases the woman, unmarried is supporting the man, while working and caring for children. The ability for her to stay home while the husband works is long gone. The pool in which women could be found by a one-woman man is diminishing. Men are often the subject of a number of women's attention, which lessen his desires to settle down. Thus the unfortunate thought: there are no good men left.

The men are either homosexual, in prison, or in the grave. And their widows made no lamentation ~ fathers not in the house raising their children has become the norm and no one seems to be sad about it. Why is that? How could an entire generation function without the leadership of a father in the home? When did it become acceptable for men to leave and have the mother fend for their children? An enemy has done this.

I read an article in a financial magazine that suggests the welfare system is positioned to emasculate men. The woman isn't able to obtain assistance if she is married and independent of the man. Thus, making the need for a husband an option, not a necessity. This says to society to shack up, make babies, but don't marry or have active fathers because if you do, help will not be awarded to you in difficult times. We are making bastardized lifestyles the norm. Young men are being raised by their mothers and the mothers are beginning to think there is no need for a man.

I am watching young men that are unable to articulate how they feel, look down to the floor when spoken to and nodding their heads to answer. Yet, they seem to feel safe and secure when their mothers are around. One evening I ran into a man I knew at a restaurant. He was with his son and told him who I was. As he did, I noticed the son had his head to the ground. I said to him, "Hold your head up son." When I said it, the father held his head up. I can't blame the boy for what he has learned nor can I blame his father. I blame the man that taught him. They aren't aware that society has already written them off because of this. The lack of confidence to look someone in the eyes is a sign of weakness. Young men should have the strong fortitude to make eye contact, speak with authority, and carry themselves as such. They walk around with hunched over backs. They sit slouched in chairs instead of straight up. People are watching and making assumptions on what they see in these young men. With no one to show them how a man should uphold himself, they learn from their mothers. This, not always, leads to boys growing up and having female like tendencies. If there was a man in the house, he could cover his son with his presence by showing him the ways of a man. Without a male role model, they mimic their sole provider: their mother. There's a generation scratching where they don't itch.

Somewhere we have to get back to where, if two people like each other, in accordance with the Bible, it is better to marry than to burn. This doesn't mean burn in the sense of going to hell, but to burn with desire. Some men say, "Well, I love her but I don't want to marry her." Well, if you have two or three children with her, you should make it a point to marry her. Young girls see this as a functioning life that she could look forward too. No one is telling them that it is best to wait until they are married to procreate. No one is telling them it is better to be an example instead of a statistic. They are perpetuating a cycle, which no one is encouraging them not to do. Where are the mothers that tell their daughter, "Be better than me instead of like me?"

So why do we miss victory in some things? It is because an enemy has sown into us things that cause us to be fearful, have our young men slack off, and our young girls fall. The enemy has caused the sanctification of families to be thrown out like trash. An enemy has done this. Men have lost their roles. It's not due to homosexuality, but by lack of responsibility.

After I read the Scripture, which I also read in Luke, what's accruing is people want relationships without relating. You have to be able to relate to the person that you're with. If you can't, then you shouldn't date. Someone might say, "Well, I did have a relationship. We were intimate." No, that's fusion. You fused together, but that's not a relationship. Your body doesn't know personality. It only wants satisfaction from another body. Your flesh doesn't respond to emotion nor does it know the difference between Lisa and Lola or Bill and Bob. To relate to someone you have to have a soul connection. We engage each other to do so. We need a deeper intimacy. Intimacy means: into me see.

An enemy has done this.

See, when people come to church, they want a word that is anodal instead of confrontational. They want a word that makes them feel good instead of one that tells them, "You can't do this and make it." People make comments like, "The church should be more loving." Love isn't the problem, discipline is. There is a lot of sampling of cookies being handed out. The standard should be set that there is no sampling if you don't plan to buy. An enemy has done this.

A television show has become very popular among women where the main character is the lover of the president. It promotes that particular lifestyle as being success. The theme is the same all around. The idea is you don't have to be upright and moral, just make money by any means. What happened to the Queens of Sheba, the Martha's, the prophet Debra's? What happened to those kinds of women? So now, the example of success is being the other one. Our children view this perversion and think it is the norm. Young girls see this as a functioning life that she could look forward too. No one is telling them that it is best to wait until they are married to procreate. No one is telling them it is better to be an example instead of a statistic. They are perpetuating a cycle, which no one is encouraging them not to do. Where are the mothers that tell their daughter, "Be better than me instead of like me"?

An enemy has done this.

People are living with noxious people in their lives. Noxious folks are those that are detrimental to your moral and physical development and cause harm to you physiology and spiritually. It is so prevalent that you give birth to what you have become. What you manifest is not seen in your behavior, but in your offspring and in your prosperity. An enemy has done this because men were asleep.

One question I asked is, is this the fault of sleeping men or the devil? Well, I think it's a combination of the two. Jesus goes into detail explaining what the parable means in Matthew 13:36. Let's see how that comes to be. If you noticed, I've been referring to the sons and daughters, people in the church, the multitude, and disciples. In the Bible, it says Jesus sent the multitude away and went into the house. The multitude is only around for the news and noise. They're pastoral followers, meaning they only come to church if the pastor is there. They'll come to church, see the pastor isn't there and leave. What they fail to realize is God will use anyone to deliver a word that will change their lives in an unchanging world. It would be better for people to stay and wait on the Lord to see what He has to say, versus leaving because they don't think they'll hear God. The multitude are also people coming for an experience with Jesus and not a relationship with Him. They often find themselves attending church for temporary repairs to their situation. "My marriage is falling apart. I guess I better go to church and get a prayer." It takes more than one night of having the church pray for them concerning their marriage. A relationship with Jesus will mend what is broken and make it whole again.

Some use the church as a hospital and come when they are in a place where friends nor family can help. "My doctor said I have months to live. I need someone to lay hands on me." Well, if the relationship was intact, they could lay hands on themselves and say, "This sickness is not unto death, but for the glory of God, that the Son of God may be glorified through it." (John 11: 4). Even so much as to remind God of His promise of, "And by His stripes [I] am healed" (Isaiah 53:5), if they had a relationship with Him and could seek His faithfulness on their own.

Verses 37 and 38 of Matthew 13 explain that the one who sows is himself, the field is the world, the good seeds are the sons of the kingdom, and the tares are the sons of the enemy. We are apt to ask God, "Why don't you take these bad people from my life?" Here's the answer: He will not take them away because you need them to grow. Imagine what lessons and strengths you would have missed had certain people not been in your life. Boldness, courage, or determination would cease to exist in you had those people not been there to raise hell in your life. You wouldn't have the drive you do to succeed had someone not told you what you'd never be able to accomplish. Their words shifted gears in you for you to prove, not only to them, but to yourself that you are capable to do all things through Christ Jesus who strengthens you. You need them for you. No matter how saved you are, you will not be exempt from dealing with non-believers. There are Christian who will not deal with anyone unlike themselves – being of the same faith. Jesus said to, "...make friends of yourselves by unrighteous mammon..."

If all your connections, contacts, friends, and family are saved, filled with the Holy Ghost then you could be missing out on some things. God will use non-believers to bless you without them knowing why they want to bless you. There could be an unsaved business man waiting in the wind to say to you, "You know, I don't know why I want to extend this offer to you, but I'll help you get your business off the ground." Your saved friends may not be able to offer you the same, but the unsaved can. God used an unbelieving woman to hide the spies of Joshua until they could get away. Had they said to her, "Nope, we'll find someone who believes in our God," they would have been killed. All your blessings and next level rises will not always come from someone who knows the Lord. It could be anyone God deems necessary for your advancement according to His will for your life.

Some people in your life and in my life aren't only there to be a soul to be won for the sake of the kingdom. They are there to be sympathizers to our faith. God used an sympathizing woman to kill the enemy of Israel, a jackass prophesied to the prophet and made an axe head swim back to the handle. He uses all kinds of things that are not saved.

The seed is the children of the kingdom whom he planted in the field – the world. You're in the world but not of the world so you should not have the same anxiety as the world. If your biological clock is ticking your faith should lead you to remember that if He did it for Sarah, He will do it for you. If you're stricken with an ailment in your loins, your faith should tell you that since He healed them, while on the earth, than He can heal me from heaven. Children of the kingdom should know from which their help comes. It comes from the hill, but the hill can send help you've never thought it would send.

There was a man by the name of Oral Roberts who spoke a prophecy saying that if he didn't get four-million dollars in so many days, God was going to call him home. God used an unsaved, rich racetrack owner to sow into his life because he sympathized with his faith. The church was in an uproar about it. "He took money from a gambler, my God the horror." Every time you come to church, there is a gambler, liar, adulteress, and conspirators to crime sowing into the Christian kingdom. I'm not referring to what people used to be. I'm saying they are in the church now. There are people who don't trust God, so they gamble on Him. When you don't return your tithe, you're telling God you have nothing that week that belongs to Him. Do you think the church would say, "All the trouble makers, we don't want your money." If that was the cases, churches would be out of business.

An enemy has done this.

I'm learning that when you become distracted, the enemy comes in and sows things that shouldn't be in you. According to the Scripture, the devil has children (Matthew 13:38), which earlier in the passage Jesus refers to as tares. The harvest is the end of the world and the reapers are the angels. Hence, the wheat, despite what it has attached to it, still grows. The evil seeds are not only around the churches, they are connected to you. This means, there are some people we will not be delivered from until Judgment Day. The concept is based on this hypostasis: if we're growing in God and someone is growing in me, and the Bible declares, "Greater is He that is in me then in the world," we should have more impact on the wicked then the wicked have on us. The wicked should not influence us. We should be able to turn them from their ways and turn to God. It's not because we are better than they are. It is because we are better off. This is because our Father is God.

People have become accustomed to hearing, "The devil is in one corner and God in another and they're fighting for your soul." That couldn't be more incorrect because God is the Creator and the enemy is the creation. The creation couldn't be in the same room with the Creator and get into a fight. All He has to say is, "Give me back my breath," and suck it right out of the enemy. God says, in Isaiah 45:7, "I form the light, and create darkness; I make peace, and create evil. I the Lord do these things." The devil doesn't have as much authority as we give him. We know this because he waited until the watchmen were asleep to sow the tares. We say things like, "The devil is on my street." Than a friend replies, "Yea, the devil was at my house too." Here's the problem with that, the enemy is not like God. He is not omnipresent like God is. We say it was the devil that destroyed something when it was a bad decision that did it.

An enemy has done this.

The Bible says God did not give us the spirit of fear. You wouldn't believe how many have trepidation when it comes to God. They worry about their job, their marriage, and their house. They are just scared, but He hasn't given us that spirit. He gave us a spirit of power, spirit of love, and a sound mind. It means you should have capacity to know what you're dealing with and be cool and calm while dealing with it. It's not that you think you're all that. It simply means, if God is for you, who could be against you? Who is bad enough to come against you if God is for you? See, God asked the question and He wants you to find the impossible answer. There is nobody who can come against you. As a true believer, you don't have to worry about who is against you, but Who is for you. And if God is for you, He'll work everything out for your good. He won't put more on you than you can bear because He's for you. If He's for you, He'll make your enemy your footstool. If you follow Him, He'll give you peace with your enemy. If God were for you, you'll have favor whether they like it or not. If God be for you, you are more than conquer. You live better than you've ever lived because God is for you. Time can't be against you because God is for you. He did it for Hezekiah and for Abraham and Sarah.

Tell yourself, "I'm going through, but I won't get stuck." The same God that can bring you to it, is the same God that can bring you through it. How do you know? David said, "Yea, though I walk through the valley of the shadow of death, I will fear no evil; for you are with me…" In other words, "I'm just walking through death. I don't live here. I'm not afraid because I know who is with me." David gets bold enough to face fear and declare he wouldn't be afraid of it. He knew that God was for him so nothing could come against him.

While men slept, an enemy came. Don't sleep when you should be focused on what is in front of you. If you're not watching your family than who is? If you're not building a relationship with God, than with whom are you building your life upon? What happens while men sleep? They wake up wondering how things happened. The world you know doesn't look, feel, nor sound the same. The enemy came in and planted seed because someone didn't find you significant enough to watch over. While men slept, children lost their innocence. The enemy not only came to steal from you, but to mess up your future. You lose your zeal and purpose, while men sleep. He'll give you stuff to destroy you, to bind you to the point you lose your dependence on God. You'll think you're doing so well and forget to give God the honor and glory for it all.

An enemy has done this.

One way to combat what the enemy has done is to value what you have. What provokes people to fall into temptations is to devalue what they have. You can take back from the enemy by celebrating the little or much in your life. You might think, "I'm about to lose my mind." I say to you, whatever you have left, praise God with it. If you're not careful you'll think what you have is nothing. When in fact, it is everything you need at this time.

But an enemy has done this.

"Even with the children birthed out of wedlock, you'll grow. In spite of what they did to you, I'll still let you grow. In spite of the three divorces, dropping out of school, not having a college education, you'll grow. You'll learn from your decisions and choices. They'll make you wiser and stronger. If you faint not, you'll be victorious over this and all things that come against you. I am your God, the One who will never leave you. Tell Me, who is like Me and who is bold enough to come against you?" --God

Let's pray.

Father, I thank You for the revelation of what the enemy has come to kill, steal, and destroy. Thank You for showing me that he has attempted to steal my family, kill my lively hood and destroy my faith in You. Father, I ask now that I am made aware of the trick of the enemy and able to come against them with Your word, which is my sword. Give me the ability to overcome what he has done knowing that it was only to hinder what it is you have me to do for your kingdom and block what I am to receive by Your grace. In Jesus' name, Amen.

8 THE SOUND OF A STRANGE PRAISE

11 And it came to pass, as he went to Jerusalem, that he passed through the midst of Samaria and Galilee. 12 And as he entered into a certain village, there met him ten men that were lepers, which stood afar off: 13 And they lifted up their voices, and said, Jesus, Master, have mercy on us. 14 And when he saw them, he said unto them, Go shew yourselves unto the priests. And it came to pass, that, as they went, they were cleansed. 15 And one of them, when he saw that he was healed, turned back, and with a loud voice glorified God, 16 And fell down on his face at his feet, giving him thanks: and he was a Samaritan. 17 And Jesus answering said, Were there not ten cleansed? but where are the nine? 18 There are not found that returned to give glory to God, save this stranger.19 And he said unto him, Arise, go thy way: thy faith hath made thee whole. Luke 17:11-19

11 And when Peter was come to himself, he said, Now I know of a surety, that the Lord hath sent his angel, and hath delivered me out of the hand of Herod, and from all the expectation of the people of the Jews. Acts 12:11

I want to talk to you about the sound of a strange praise. The backdrop of this text is more complicated than it appears. The assumption within it is that the ten lepers were somehow related. They are classified as a group and it appears as though they have been together all the time. However, there is mix culture amongst the lepers. One was different from the rest – that one was a Samaritan.

At this time, in the Bible, a Samaritan was an Arabic person who is not only of two races but also of three. The name means difficult or hard to love. When Jesus dealt with the woman that was Samaritan, he called her a dog. Her response was, 'Yes, Lord, yet even the little dogs under the table eat from the children's crumbs," (Mark 7:27-28 NKJV). He said to her, "For this saying go your way; the demon has gone out of your daughter," You have to learn to trust God even when you're insulted. When you read the text of the leper Samaritan, you'll see that in the mix culture there is at least one stranger.

Now what brings at least one or a group of people together who have no culture? Well, they are diseased. According to the law of the Levites, you have to be disconnected from everyone else and have to announce you are coming. "The unclean is coming! I'm unclean! Leper coming!" This was because everything you touched became unclean. Nevertheless, even unwanted people want company. Here we have ten unwanted men who have no common background, yet they emulate each other's existence and find people with similar struggles. While they are together, you'll see something happen. The one that comes back gets an 'aha' moment. He reaches a critical point of recognition. This happens when you get a peek of something that is at a far distance from where you are. For when it's dark as can be and you see a ray of light, it lets you know this soon will pass. It is important to understand because when you experience it, it appears to be hope. Yet, it is much greater than hope. It's letting you recognize something that you know can happen. In other words, if you've never seen light, you couldn't appreciate the light. The fact you know what it looks like, you can start praising God for it.

The critical point of recognition tells you something is about to change. Sometimes God will not give you the whole picture, He'll give you preview. In those moments of revelation, your whole life begins to change. Things that seem like they were dead come alive because the life that is in front of you comes back to your present. You start to realize that everything around you will not always be the way it is. When God gives you a preview, your praise becomes a little different. You've experienced what He has in store and it becomes just enough for you to become prepared for what is to come.

The Bible says when Jesus came into a certain village, the lepers stood off afar knowing they couldn't get close to Him. They lifted up their voice and said, "Jesus have mercy on us." One thing you will notice here is Jesus did not lay hands on them to help them. All He did was send a Word their way. Some people think you have to lay hands on everyone to be healed, but all you need is a Word of God to change your illness into a lesson. When Jesus saw them, this is how they got their healing, "Go show yourself to the priest." What got them delivered? Obedience. After you have passed your season of leprosy, your season of disease the priest has to declare you are no longer unclean. What I love is, the Bible says as they went to the priest they were cleansed. Not as they were coming back from the priest but as they were going to the priest. Don't you know you can never run from God but you can run to him? As you get closer to God, stuff that had a hold on you will begin to fall off because it can't stand the presence of God. As they went, they were cleanse.

Hebrew history says that at least seven of them were Jewish. You would think that with 10 of them in the group, seven of them being church people would know what to do. Yet, it was a Samaritan that knew what to do in the presence of the Lord. As he saw that he was no longer infected, he went back to give God glory. He was the one deemed hard to love and an outsider. He turned back and with a loud voice gave God glory. The Bible says Jesus calls him a stranger. Please note the sound of a strange praise. The people who should have been given Him glory got their healing, but forgot their praise. However, the man who you would never have expected, the one you least believe in had enough sense to realize if it was not for Him, he wouldn't have been healed. Even though he didn't know Jesus as his Lord and Savior, I do know He healed my body. Jesus may not have known him, but he knew Jesus understood praise. And he came back to give Him glory. Jesus was expecting the ones who knew him to give him glory.

It's a strange praise to give God glory in the midst of a messy situation.

That's not expected of you. People don't expect you to give God praise when you're going through a tough time. Nobody stops in the middle of his or her trial to give God praise unless you know God is with you in the middle of whatever you're going though. People often give him praise after deliverance. No one in his or her right mind would, in the middle of drowning, lift their hands, open their mouth and give God glory. That's a strange praise. But if you know that strange praise is the best praise, you'll do it. It's the one you least expect. Even if it's not going your way, you give Him praise. If He heals or He doesn't, you give him praise. Nobody expects you to thank Him, but you need to make up your mind to give Him praise anyways.

It's called *Samaritanism* when you help and/or celebrate someone else, yet are unknown. When people don't know your name but still want to help. To the church, it is called the "Insult of Samaritanism." The insult is that the Samaritan is beating us in showing love. We are getting what we want from God but not giving to anyone else. But the strange person, who is that? The drug dealer and the lesbian are the strange people. The Bible says as they went they were cleansed. Don't stop anyone from coming into the church with his or her *stuff*. Once they step over the threshold, their baggage turns into garbage. When the garage comes in, He will be a consuming fire. Even though you are judging them, they are giving God more praise and glory than those that are supposed to.

Some people are coming to God and coming out of some stuff. They are walking out of something that has been with them a long time. They are being cleansed of what has held on to them with no intentions of letting go. The strange praise comes from those that don't know God like seasoned saints and believers. The praise is supposed to come from those that know Him. There are strangers coming that are going to say stuff like, "Man that dude was preaching and telling the truth." If someone hears him, he'll say, "We don't talk like that here." He's a stranger; he has no idea of what to say. "I'm a stranger and what I learned is God will hear the sound of a strange praise. I don't know who your Bishop is, what a missionary is, I don't know what a district is or even what a pastor is, but I do know I once was lost, but now I'm found."

Please believe the strangers are coming. They're coming in and praising God the only way they know how. If popping and locking is all they know, let them do it. If fist pumping is their thing, let them do it. "Oh no, we don't praise like that in this church." They're not coming to church. They're coming to God. The sound of a strange praise.

Jesus said, "Where are the nine? There were 10 of you." The Samaritan didn't have a response. In fact, Jesus answered his own question when He said, "There were none to be found to give glory to God except this stranger." Here's why the Samaritan never answered Jesus' question, it wasn't because he didn't have anything to say. While Jesus was talking, he was praising. You have to get to a place in your walk where you learn to praise God by yourself. While folks are trying to destroy your future, praise God. If someone is lying about you, give God praise. While they are planning against you, praise God. The next voice in the Scripture was Jesus. He told him, "Go your way. Your faith has made you whole." In other words, "You did what I asked by going to show yourself to the priest. Now because of your faith and obedience, you can go your way." This means if you listen to God and do as He commands of you, He will send you on your way healed from all that plagues you.

In Acts 12:11 — they were praying for Peter and going through the motions. See, if people don't show up on time, you think it's over, but it's not. The Scripture says, "And when Peter had come to himself, he said, "Now I know for certain that the Lord has sent His angel, and has delivered me from the hand of Herod and from all the expectations of the Jewish people." I'm telling you, if you learn to trust God, He will deliver you from the expectations of other people. They expect you to die, but you live. They expect you to fall out, but you stand up. They're expecting you to cry, but you're laughing. When the expectation is for you to give up, God gives you what you need to keep going. That's why you need to let your praise be loud and even obnoxious. Let them know it isn't over for you.

Despite all that you've been through, your praise lets the naysayers and doubters know you are still alive. It's a strange praise to them because after all you've been through, you still have your praise—as strange praise! It's a strange praise when they hear muffling from the ground from where they thought they had buried you. However, they can't bury your praise. If you keep giving God praise while their hand is on you and their foot on your neck, your praise will fight for you.

Let's pray.

Father, I come to You with worship in my hands and a strange praise in my mouth. Father, teach me to praise You despite what it looks like, sounds like, or what I think it is. I know that as long as You are with me nothing can come against me. So, I praise You now in the middle of my storm for in it You are watering my seeds of faith, blowing debris from my life and washing me clean. Thank You for hearing the tears of my heart and the screams of my eyes and my silent cries. I give You glory through it all, in Jesus' name. Amen.

9 IT'S CALLED RESPECT

The book of Isaiah chapter 3 was a continuum of chapter 2 in the original text. When the scholars tried to categorize the Bible and broke it down into segments they left this section as it is now. In Chapter 2 God has a struggle with His own people because they decide to trust in man instead of in Him. For the whole chapter He listens to their request and watches as they slight Him as their only Resource. He responds to their rebellion in chapter 3. Now, the first 5 verses in chapter 3, God is simply saying to His people, "It's called respect."

In the Western culture, we tend to redefine words and as a result, the American English language has been deemed the laziest in the world! We have smashed words together such as abuse, which is actually abnormal use. The original term for good morning and good night was God be in your morning and God be in your night. It digressed from God be in your morning to Good morning to Morning. Nowadays, morning has been reduced to, "What's up" which been smashed to 'Sup. In the last decade or so, the basic greeting has modified from spoken salutations to a simple head nod. The reason this is important is because God says to His people in essence, "You're showing me no respect."

The first definition of respect is to pay attention to detail, to observe, to discern. To be overlooked is to be disrespected. We use it as, "Don't disrespect me," which is the only definition most know. It's not only disrespect by what someone says, it is also what they do. If someone comes in the room and extends their hand to you, yet you don't take it, that's a form of disrespect. Sometimes people can be full of ignorance and it would be more disrespectful for you to respond to their idiocy. Don't become engaged with something in which you have to lower your dignity and other people can't tell which person is the idiot.

Sometimes you have to be too noble to respond to certain people and their idiosyncratic behavior… It's called respect!

Often time, we don't realize there is a broad gap between obedience and blessing, sin and judgment. However, the church has the propensity to make them closer. We say things like, "If I'm obedient God should bless me." There's a broad gap because God doesn't want you to serve Him for His gift. He doesn't want you to live right because of what you can get. He wants you to live right because you know you're supposed to. See, if you do right based on the consequence for doing wrong, you're still not right. If you said, "Well, I'm not going to sin because I don't want to go to hell," your motives to do right are not legit. To do right wouldn't be your core value, not going to hell would be. Your righteousness doesn't come with consequences. If there was no heaven or hell, you should still want to do what's righteous.

Understand that there's a great gulf between obedience and blessing, which is why people become discouraged in church. You can see someone who just joined receive a huge blessing compared to yourself who has been in the church for twenty something years. You'll think God should bless you because you've been around for so long, but He doesn't work that way. He blesses whomever He desires and delays whomever He desires to delay. You can't expedite his hand by naming it and claiming it because you can't provoke God to respond to your time schedule! On the other hand, the Bible says He's slow to wrath and longsuffering. If He wasn't longsuffering there would be a smaller gap between sin and judgment! He would be an unfair God if He had a small gap for blessing and obedience and a wide gap for sin and judgment. You have to do something wrong for a long time to have God come in. That's why if you mess up you have to get up and ask God for forgiveness within that long and broad space He gives!

Not everyone can testify to this: you will never have to tell on some people because they've gotten to a place in God that they know what makes them. They know they are strong and weak, smart and dumb, brave and scary. They know that God loves them in their right and wrong. They tell on themselves because they respect God.

Any time you come to church and you lose your joy and can't get happy because of some person, you're basically telling God, "This person has more impact in my life than You." No one should have the influence to have your joy in their hand. There is nobody on this planet to have enough authority to take your joy. The joy you have, the world didn't give it so the world can't take it away! If you lose your job and can't praise God, you're telling Him you have more respect for your job than you do for Him. If you know the Lord is your Shepherd and you shall not want, lack or go without, you know there are other opportunities, but never another God. Sure it hurts, but the God we serve is able to do above all that we can ask or think. God says, "Since you don't want to obey me I'm going to turn you over to man." It's called respect!

Be careful who you give respect to first. In the first passage of Isaiah,

He takes away the support of the people. The stay and staff is the support system. He says, "I'm the one that supplies your bread and water." When the dust settles you'll realize man doesn't provide for you, God does. Be careful not to boast about how hard you worked for something. "I worked hard for this and that." That could be true, but if God didn't give you the grace to do it, you wouldn't have or be where you are! People tend to make a fatal illogicalities after receiving what they asked God for. He blesses you with a new job after being without one for some time. Now, that you have the job you prayed, fasted, and gave an offering for, you don't have time to come to God's house. He blesses you with a new car. When you didn't have the car you made your way to church by any means necessary! After the car is acquired, all of a sudden you can't make it for this and that reason. What you're telling God is, "I have more respect for the material than the Messiah." If you really want to make God angry, put something in front of Him. Have something in your life that you worship and praise more than you do Him. He said in His word, "I AM a jealous God. Jealousy is My name." He will take away everything that you decide is greater than He is. Let me show you His jealousy. In the temple there was a god named Magog whom they placed next to the ark of the covenant. Three chapters later they returned to the temple to find Magog knocked over. Five verses later they set Magog back up only to later find him with his head cut off. God doesn't want another god next to, behind, or in front of Him. Hence, why He warned that He is a jealous God and Jealousy is His name. That is why you should be careful being a part of an ecumenical fellowship. If the banner is not blood stained, don't be under it! Crescent moon and star, Buddhism, Jehovah's Witness or Seventh day Adventistism aren't blood stained. He has to be God of all or He's not God at all!

It's called respect!

If you forget where your help comes from, He's going to remind you. He says, "I'm going to take away your bread and water. Let me see what you do when you trust in man. I'm that One that provides for you. But now you want to trust in man, let Me take away what I do." He gave you the ability to get what you need. He's saying, "I'm going to take away the mighty men in your life." Mighty men are men of courage. God needs mighty men in your life to keep you lifted up. He put them in your life to bless you. Nevertheless, in the Scripture He is saying, "Since you want to do things your way, I'll take away my hand. I'll take away judges and prophets." You need people who love you but will make a judgment decision. If you want to put your trust and respect in man, He'll take away all that He's doing to allow you to see that it was Him all along.

He hand picks people to be in your life to make you sharp. Some of us wouldn't be around the people we are now if God hadn't connected them to us. You said, "God have your way," and He had His way, which led certain people to you. When you allow Him to have His way, He moves things around in your favor. One of the reasons many people are in the conditions they're in is that they failed to trust God.

An example would be giving someone a promotion in the church because of his or her monetary gifts. It's done without consulting God because they don't trust Him to sustain the church. What can happen is promotions are given to those who are gifted but nasty, have resources but not integrity, ability but no moral compass. It's called respect!

When God says He'll remove the honorable men from your life, He's saying the people that keep you in check will be removed. Honorable people give you balance and challenge your integrity. You will not do some things in front of an honorable person. When you have those kinds of people in your life, you'll think twice about doing something ungodly. He'll take away productive people in your life. That's why the Bible says two are better than one and a threefold cord is not easily broken. You were going to say something but decided to bite your tongue because you had honorable people around you.

I can tell where you are going by whom you are connected to just by seeing your contacts in your phone.! You're not going to go any further than those connections! If everyone in your phone is on the same economical level, you'll never increase. If you don't have people in your contacts that double your income, you're not going anywhere! If all your counselors are your age, you aren't going anywhere! You need people in your life on different intellectual levels! They are where you should strive to be. You need to see where you're going by connecting with people who are already there!

It's called respect. Respect - be discerning and pay attention to whom you're talking to.

People become offended when you become something without them. That's why they will not show you respect. They don't know your "now" they only know your "used to be." When Jesus speaks, they name everything He used to be, but never who He is. Most people who can't comprehend what you have become, identify with you retrospectively! Because they had nothing to do with your success, they try to belittle who you are. Nevertheless, allow them to be disappointed, because when God elevates you, toleration is not an option, celebration is! No one else gets the credit!

When they tried to disrespect Jesus, the Bible says, "He went around into another city." When there is no respect, go around!

In verse number 11, Jesus explains what to do when people don't respect you. He calls the disciples to give them the power they'll need on their journeys (verse 7). He told them to shake the dust off their shoes when someone doesn't receive what they have to offer. Leave the dust as a reminder that they were there. The same goes for you. Don't take the disrespect from others to your next experience or next relationship. Leave it where it was – on the ground.

It's called respect.

Don't lose sleep over folks who don't know who you are. Even if it's family, church family, old friends or new friends. If they don't know, don't become upset, just keep moving as Jesus did. They will find out in due time. God said He will make your name great. Since He will make your name great, those that don't know you now, will know you later. Go about your life rest assured that God knows who you were then, who you are now and who you'll be later!

You may be at the crossroad of uncertainty and say to yourself, "I have put some things in front of God and I forgot about Him." Give your life to God. Let Him show you how to keep Him first. Allow Him to correct you if you forget. He said in His word, "All those who keep their mind on Me will remain in perfect peace." Come to God to receive your peace. You deserve it. He's waiting for you to make up your mind. Don't wait for another time or your significant other. If you do, you're telling God that time and man/woman is in front of Him. Respect what God is saying to you. God wants you to have a brand new beginning in Him. You have the opportunity of a lifetime, but you only have the lifetime of the opportunity! Make the step towards Christ now.

When you become saved, you're a believer. You become a Christian when your lifestyle changes. Are you ready to change your lifestyle?

Let's pray.

Lord, this is where I am. I got caught up and put some things in front of You. I love You Lord, but I have to be honest with myself and You. I disrespected You by putting other things in front. Father, I give you glory and praise. Thank You for the word that spoke to me with specificity. If you take away my bread and stay, my support, I will not make it. God, I repent for my wrongdoings. Forgive me, in the name of Jesus. God, I return to my first love, which is You, like never before. In Jesus' name, amen and amen.

10 YOU HAVE AN APPOINTMENT WITH A GIANT

1 Samuel 17: 34-37- And David said unto Saul, Thy servant kept his father's sheep, and there came a lion, and a bear, and took a lamb out of the flock: And I went out after him, and smote him, and delivered it out of his mouth: and when he arose against me, I caught him by his beard, and smote him, and slew him. Thy servant slew both the lion and the bear: and this uncircumcised Philistine shall be as one of them, seeing he hath defied the armies of the living God. David said

moreover, The Lord that delivered me out of the paw of the lion, and out of the paw of the bear, he will deliver me out of the hand of this Philistine. And Saul said unto David, Go, and the Lord be with thee.

Say to yourself, "I have an appointment with a giant." Are you ready for what you are about to face?

The first thing I want to establish, which might go against what you've learned in Sunday school and during the years you attended church, is this: Goliath was not a Philistine. This is important to point out because if he were a part of the Philistines, he would fight with them against Israel. He said to Israel, "Send out man that we may fight together..." He never said send an army to fight him. He is a soloist—he fights one on one. He is what's called a champion, which in the Hebrews text literally means one who fights in between the camps. The Bible says the Philistines stood on one side of the mountain while Israel stood on the opposite side with a valley between them. That's where Goliath stood. That's what giants do; they don't fight in groups they fight alone. How do you fight? This is important to know and understand because some of us are not going to have battles on the mountaintops nor on someone else's valley. Some of our battles will be as we go. Some will be in between your promotion and your firing – in between camps. Some fights will be between your family and church family. If you don't know how to fight in between camps, you don't know which camp to be in, in the first place. See, whenever God comes in, He doesn't come in to take sides. He comes in and takes over!

To understand how much of a giant Goliath was, take a look at what he was equipped with. The Bible uses shekels as a Hebrew derivative to measure pounds and ounces. His coat weighed 157lbs and the spearhead of his weapon was 18lbs. He had targets, also referred to as javelins, in between his shoulders. He's equipped with three types of weapons: a sword, spears and javelins. He came ready to kill, not to be killed. His shield was so heavy he had a man carrying it. He was approximately 9½ feet tall! That should give you an idea as to what David was up against at that time.

Remember, Goliath was from the land of Gath, which is in the City of Philistia. Again, he wasn't a Philistine. They just claimed him. He was from the tribe of Avvim who were dark skin people. He had a wide nose and flat forehead. Unlike the Nordic giants who were of the Viking origins, with slanted heads. That's good to know that Goliath was not a Nordic giant, had David slung his rock at him, it would have slid off his head! However, God designed a weapon for David that would hit a flat faced giant right in the middle of his head. God will have your weapon tailor made for your worries!

Now in 1 Samuel 17:20-23, David arrived to the fight cheering the army on as he did what his father commanded of him. He went to find his brothers, but while he was there, he asked a question that they didn't like. He inquired of the prize for killing the giant. None of the soldiers was thinking about killing Goliath, they were just trying to survive. Here's the challenge: David is the smallest one at the battle.

Nevertheless, when he gets there something incredible happens. For forty days, Goliath was selling wolf tickets to the army of Israel. He was bullying them until, in verse 23 on the forty-first day, David heard him. That was Goliath's fatal mistake. Now what makes David hearing him so important? How can David hear him if he is moving through the crowd cheering Israel on? Often times we run from what appears as though we can't handle. However, God knows just what we need to get us to tackle that which we run from. To do that, he allows us to hear certain words. Some things you think are hurtful words, God wanted you to hear. You have to hear some things to trigger who you are. You wouldn't have stepped into who you are if you hadn't heard certain things. Some have to hear you'll never be anything or you'll never make it. Some things you wish you never heard were the trigger you needed to move forward and do it. Some said you'll never have a business, so you spent nights burning the candle on both ends to create your business plan. You need to hear you can't so you can. You need to hear what you can't do to push you to what God is able to help you do. The Bible says that with God all things are possible. What did you hear that made you prepare for your greatness?

David heard him say what they could and could not do. In the 14 chapters where giants are mentioned, seven in 1st Samuel and seven 2nd Chronicles, the giants never spoke to anyone. The only reason he is speaking now, specifically to David, is because David had something in him the others didn't have. Some giants are only going to talk when you show up. You'll know it's your time when the giant you face starts talking! In versus 24 and 25, David's own brothers see something on him. When they should have been angry at the problem they faced, they were angry with him. David was asking questions that others weren't asking. He was thinking different. When you don't think like others, they'll start to think you're full of yourself. That's not the case at all. You're just stepping up to another level. You see things differently, from a different vantage point, so you respond and ask questions unlike those around you. Get ready to face your giant!

When David asked about the price for killing the giant, he was brought before the king. Looking at his size, he automatically dismissed David. However, David stood up and told him that what he faced in his own backyard was the same size as what Israel was facing. Whatever you're going to face, you'll be prepared for! Nothing will be a surprise to you because you've defeated it before! David went to the battle with five smooth stones. It was what he carried with him because he never knew what he would face. Your stones should be the word of God. Whatever you face in life, there is a word from God to get you through!

You have an appointment with a giant only if you're a giant! The only way you're going to face big things is you have to be big. Nobody is going to face a giant with a small mindset. You can't get giant advice from little people. You can't tell me how to deal with this issue if you don't have giant in your DNA. David was small in stature, but big in God. He was the only one to talk back to the giant. The giant shifts the conversation from the wind to David. David said to him, "Just as I killed the lion and bear I'm going to cut your head off." He doesn't laugh or brush Goliath off, because there was a giant in David. Giants are only going to show up when you do. You can be in a place but if you're not in a place with God the giant in you will not show up! You're not significant enough. As you begin to grow in God, giants show up because you can conquer everything else. If you were worried about your income, you're not a giant. When you are a giant you have big things on your mind. You don't worry about daily bread because you prayed about it. God said He is your daily bread.

In 1 Samuel 21:9 after David killed Goliath, and the sword he used to take off his head was available, he said, "There is none like that, give it to me." Riddle me this, if Goliath was almost ten feet tall, his coat is one hundred fifty pounds, the spearhead is eighteen pounds, a shield so big he has a servant carrying it, what size is his sword? Better yet, how big is David? How could David feel comfortable with a giant sword? This is the same sword Goliath showed up with and that David used to kill him. Somewhere along the battle he left the sword, this is later gift-wrapped for the giant. You're wondering, who's the giant? The giant is David! There's a giant in David that told him he needed what Goliath had. When something seems like it's made just for you, it probably is!

After he kills him, no one gives him a parade. No one was excited when David did something that was impossible. His brothers didn't celebrate him. They were mad because of his success. When you become blessed, not everyone is going to celebrate with you. Be careful whom you share your victories with because some will understand the violence that you suffered for your victory!

When you're a giant, you're an easy target. Giants are easy to talk about, easy to dog out and easy to see! You can't hide if you wanted to because you're big. You're too big not to be seen. Everybody knows what you're doing because you're big – big in God. That's why some of you are losing your joy because you're a giant holding a little person's hand. You know you're a giant when you can walk into a room and not feel intimidated. You don't have to be tall to be a giant. You don't have to big in physicality when you're big in God. Believing God for big things is for giants! There's nothing wrong with aspiring for great things. Some want to be blessed so they can bless the kingdom!

When you are a giant, a giant will see you. Why would God take his people to a land flowing with milk and honey with giant stuff? Because the God we serve is bigger than what we believe. Do you think God wants to give a bunch of small people giant food? If you know you're a giant, tell somebody, "I'm a giant! I only show up when battle calls me." You have an appointment with a giant!

Any time you have to stoop down to talk to someone, you're stepping out of your giant persona. You can have common touch, but always remember who you are!

What happened to those stones David had when he was a kid?

In 2 Samuel 21:15-19, David, later in life after thinking he was done fighting, was faced yet again with a giant issue. The Bible says David became tired during the fight and would have been killed, but he had help this time. David had men with him who killed giants! This meant they only have giant mentalities. The battles with the Philistines put them face to face with the giants. David knew he was too old to fight but he turned around and got men that got a hold of his spirit. They don't deal with little stuff only giant stuff. Read the Scriptures, his men were not giants killing giants. It was because a giant mentored them! Your appointment is not with Goliath but with David. Your David will teach you how to live big, stand up tall and how to live the giant life at only 4½ feet tall! They were killing giants left and right. See, if you don't look through the right eyes, you'll miss your giant. Like David, your giant may be small but make a big impact and change your life. What time is your appointment?

Between David and his men, five giants were killed. One was the father and other were the sons. David had stones for now and stones for later. The more you live and are with God, the more of a target you'll become. The more God uses you and blesses you, the more you'll have to use the stones you have. Get ready, you're battle is coming. God will prepare you for what is to come. Small things added to your life are for the big fights God is preparing you for. Everybody connected to David had a giant killing anointing on him or her. The giants he faced before were bigger than the one in the past. If God gives you an appointment with a giant, it's with someone to bring the giant out of you. You had better find your giant!

When your giant comes out, you'll be too big for petty things.

Nobody wants what they can't handle. However, as long as you know who you are in God, what size you are in God, you'll come up against things that will fall to your feet before the battle begins. People will wonder how you did it, but they'll never understand because they aren't giants. There are times where you will face things that others can't. Those things will come at you because God knows you can deal with it! Don't wonder, "Why me?" Instead say, "Giant, rise up. We have battle to win!" The God in you is bigger than anything you can come against. The Lord is always with you, so whatever comes against you will not prevail over you. Know that God has equipped you for a time such as this. You have to be bold like David and run at your giant. You know how to handle it. As you see big things coming your way, know God is going to set up an appointment with your giant. If you killed it before, you can kill it again. The word of God is your sword. It has giant slaying capability. It is not for killing your brothers and sisters, but it's for giant killing only!

There's something greater in you scratching to get out. It only needs to hear one thing to burst through and push you into where you're supposed to be. Don't fight it, just let it go. You have an appointment with a giant that is going to release the giant in you! What time is your appointment?

Let's pray.

Father, thank You for the giant in me. I pray I can hear something that speaks to the giant that is scratching to get out. I give You glory now for what is going to happen when it is released. I await the giant lifestyle that is waiting for me. Change my surrounds, company and way of thinking. You are the God of all things impossible. Help me to live an impossible life so that others can see, through You, that all things are possible for those who love You. I send up praises now for my later. In Jesus' name. Amen.

11 THE MAKING OF A MANLESS SOCIETY

Wherefore they are no more twain, but one flesh. What therefore God hath joined together, let not man put asunder. They say unto him, Why did Moses then command to give a writing of divorcement, and to put her away? He saith unto them, Moses because of the hardness of your hearts suffered you to put away your wives: but from the beginning it was not so. And I say unto you, Whosoever shall put away his wife, except *it be* for fornication, and shall marry another, committeth adultery: and whoso marrieth her which is put away doth commit adultery. His disciples say unto him, If the case of the man be so with *his* wife, it is not good to marry. But he said unto them, All *men* cannot receive this saying, save *they* to whom it is given. For there are some eunuchs, which were so born from *their* mother's womb: and there are some eunuchs, which were made eunuchs of men: and there be eunuchs, which have made themselves eunuchs for the kingdom of heaven's sake. He that is able to receive *it*, let him receive *it*. Matthew 19:6-12

The making of a manless society. Fundamentally speaking, the homo-erectus is the man 2 million years ago, so the anthropologists said. They stood upright and had the large protruding forehead. Then 1.5 million years ago came the East African man, the homo-habilis who had become more intellectual. Today we have the homo sapien who has learned how to communicate and use tools.

If you fall into sin in your 20's that's a fall, but if you fall in your 50's for what you fell with in your 20's, that's a failure! Somewhere you haven't matured. Some things should not be named among you in your 50's, 60's, 70's age wise, that were named among you in your teens and roaring 20's. If you have the same struggles as a teenager and 20's than you have not matured, you just got old. So what do I mean by a manless society? Well it goes beyond homosexuality.

I remember seeing the latest issue of *Essence Magazine* featuring a new show called, *Orange is the New Black*. The problem is who was featured on the cover - Laverne Cox, a transgender man. A man is on the front cover of Essence, a women's magazine. You can buy it at newsstands or subscribe to it. A man is on the front cover impersonating a woman. He also had a photo shoot in there.

Then you have *Vanity Fair* with Bruce Jenner on their front cover. Bruce said, "Call me Caitlin." They've always had women on the cover. My emphasis is not to be homophobic or transgender phobic, but what's happening is our society is losing the influence of the man.

We're watching society become androgynistic, or a unisex society. This is where you don't determine which sex is which. This ultimately is about fathers. The making of a manless society is to deemphasis masculinity from a biblical perspective and redefine it. The making of a manless society is a de emphasis on masculinity. If you redefine it, you can cause the purpose to be lost!

I remember a couple of years ago I got into a debate while I was on chairman of the board for the Black Leadership Commission on AIDS (BLACA). A man began saying, "I should have a right as a homosexual man to marry my lover. I appeared to be ignorant and asked him, "Is your lover a woman?" He said, "No he's a man." According to the confines of marriage you must have a man and a woman to constitute a marriage! You see, marriage came from the Bible, and it says it's between a man and a woman. He said he should have the same right and civil rights as an African American. "If I want to marry a man I should be able to do that," he tried to persuade me. I explained that he wanted rights for behavior! I had no choice being born African American, but marriage has parameters. If you want to be in it, you've got to fit within the parameters and confines that marriage operates in! I didn't make it up.. I'm just the messenger. One of you has to be a man, one of you has to be a woman to constitute a marriage. Opposite poles attract, like poles repel! Man is what the Hebrews call "Ish" the woman is the "Ishah" the appropriate partner - the one who fits the man!

In Matthew 19 Jesus is giving a rebuttal to the disciples because some questions arose among his followers concerning marriage. Why should men marry if they can't get divorced for any reason? Moses had to limit the definition of divorce for any and all reasons, Jesus explained. Their hearts became hardened. Men would divorce their wives for any and all reasons. They would get a divorce because they were footed, or had a lazy eye, or had stretch marks after she was pregnant.....Jesus then takes it a step further. If you go to Genesis there was no divorce. That was not God's design from the beginning. If a man divorces his wife for any other reason beside fornication/adultery, when he remarrys, he brings both he and her into adultery. Fornication here does not mean just sex before marriage but anything that is sexually immoral. This is the only basis for divorce, according to the Bible. Some were born eunuchs from their mother's womb, some were made eunuchs, and some made themselves eunuchs for the sake of the kingdom. In that commitment it's more about your will than about your emotions. If you say you are going to leave him or her, you have to have biblical grounds. Most people don't assess this before they get into marriage. They marry because they like what they see. But physical and visual displays aren't going to last forever. They may lose their six pack. Their hair may change color. Some things might become droopy, and you're going to have to decide what really matters. Did I get married for the aesthetics and what it does for me, or is my soul in this? Are you committed to following kingdom principles in marriage and respecting your husband, or loving your wife? Marriage is meant for life.

Next Jesus deals with eunuchs. Being a eunuch meant they would castrate men while they were watching. The greater danger is when you have men psychologically castrated. Here is the problem today, you have young men who have been psychologically castrated because their mothers won't allow boys to become men! The women are raising the young men, because they don't have a father. The mothers don't know how to mold and shape a man because they weren't meant to. This perpetuates the problem because the mothers are castrating their little boys and you've got to be careful because you have allowed yourself to make your little boy a demigod. Now they are sixteen and seventeen and they are not ready for the real world which is ready to chew them up and spit him out. There are young men who have graduated college but don't know how to change a tire! There are others who don't know how to balance a checkbook! They don't have responsibility or know how to pay a bill. They don't know how to take their hat off in a building or hold a door for a woman. They don't know how to pay the bill at dinner. They're trying to be cool, but being cool cannot substitute substance! We are raising a society of manless men, undeveloped men who have been psychologically castrated. The only example they have is their mother, their grandmother, and their aunt. You've got to see a man to be a man. If no one taught you, you don't know how to be a man. We have young men with no fathers, no examples, and no one to learn how to treat a woman. They don't hold a job, or be a father to the next generation. If you are a man, you need responsibility and reconciliation to God! You're a masterpiece, because you're a piece of the Master!

You've got to see a man to be a man and the problem is the mentees have no mentors. Instead, our men are being influenced by the feminine culture. Young men are wearing leggings. Our young men are wearing acrylic nails and lip liner. I am not talking about transgenderism. I am talking about young men being influenced by a feminine culture. They're fatherless, they have no role models, with no one to show them how to be a man. Bastardized by a godless society redefining purposes with proposals!

So when our men show up at church, they need to be celebrated. They don't need to be pastors or deacons or ushers or elders to be honored! They just need to be here to be celebrated, appreciated, and welcomed.

Jesus was not a man who was weak and mamby pamby. The Bible says Jesus was angry. Some of us have painted Christ of the Bible as a feminine, esoterically, Vidal Sassoon character floating through the air. The table he overturned of the money changers weighed over 475 pounds. He was a leader. He was a leader's leader. You have a man's man to get 12 men to quit their jobs, leave everything, and follow you! This is the Jesus of the Bible. You don't hear that preached in the church often...He chased them out with a whip in his hand. He is a man, but we have eunuchs. We have manless men. Man must have testicular fortitude!

Ladies, if he wants use your credit card, drive your car and live in your house, he's a boy and not a man! Someone is going to marry you one day. He can't be intimidated by your success and be around other men. Young men, you can't be asleep while your mother is doing chores that you should be doing!

When you castrate a man, you take away his drive, not just for intimacy but his drive period! When you are a eunuch, you have a man castrated to watch the harem of another king. They would castrate a man to have him watch the women without worrying about him trying to get with any of them. But even worse than this is the mental castration of a man. By this I mean to punish by severe force and brutality. Some people no longer have testicular fortitude, so the problem is young men inside and outside church that have been psychologically castrated because their mama won't let them grow up to be cowboys, the mother who is raising her son because of a deadbeat father. Some Father's Days are just that day, the day they made the baby and you never see them again. In some cases the men are not in place and the women are raising these babies. But instead of raising them, some women have turned their child into an idol worship. In that case, they will grow up and embarrass you. You won't let him fall, no one can touch him, the other boys are playing and you don't want him to play and get hurt. You've got to be careful to not allow your baby boy to be a demigod. You're castrating him and now he is 16 or 17 and he is waiting for you to make his bed and clean his clothes. He sleeps while you do the chores. You're castrating the man by doing everything for him. They've been given no responsibility and he is going to be a grown boy.

Being a responsible man makes you a priest. Women need a man of responsibility. If nobody taught you, there is no way in the world that you can be a man and have responsibility to communicate and use tools to fix things. Let me tell you what's happening in teenage and unmarried pregnancies. You have young men raised by their mother still looking for their girlfriends to mother them.

If I am going to hell I am not going to have 5 children out of wedlock. Responsibility is never put on the manless man. It's the teenage girl stuck with the baby and her mother has got to raise the baby. Now he can't just go off and do whatever he wants, he needs to go and get a job. He needs to be held accountable and responsible. We are producing a manless society where young men are not taking responsibility. When you have indifferent men, you have endorsement. If you don't respond to this pandemic and do something as a man, God will hold you responsibility. We need mentors to help these young men become the men of God they are created to be.

The Bible says some people made themselves eunuchs. It is against the law to have HIV and not let people know your status. It's like the leper in Bible times. There are men who have had transgender surgery and then they come to the Lord. You can't get back what you've cut off. You've made yourself a eunuch. You can't get married or have children.

I saw a commercial recently by the U.S. Army about a young boy at a baseball game with his father. The young boy saw the father stand up and take off his hat. He learned what to do by looking up to his father. If you can get some men to learn to look up to their father, it changes everything. If they don't have a father, there's a call to the fathers out there to father the next generation. I remember when John F. Kennedy was assassinated. His son saw the casket go by, he was no more than 3 years old and he saluted the casket. He saw what the other men were doing and he followed. I wonder, what do you see men doing today? Where did you get that behavior. Where did you pick up the spirit of irresponsibility? Late for work, late for paying their bills, late for dates. I am watching three and four year old boys with earrings in their ear. You don't even know what you are doing, you're trying to make him cool, but you're castrating him. Being a man is a call to excellence. What you do to your children, they are going to do to society.

The truth is God said, "Let us make man in our image." We are supposed to be His representative. When God made the garden He said there was not a man to til the ground. You are a homo sapien, you communicate with language and you use tools to survive. When I see deacons and ministers in here that aren't upset about seeing men going the wrong direction, I pray God doesn't give you sleep until you see the responsibility you have for the next generation.

How dare you leave your 21 year old son at home, while you come to church. "Well, I am not going to make him come to church," they say. He's in your house, eating your bread, sucking up the air in the room. Laying on the couch, big old size 14's hanging over the couch. You've got to teach that boy to be responsible and to get up. Don't sleep until noon, ever. Even if you don't have to work, you don't sleep until noon, life is calling you. Turn over the mattress, and get up. It's time to get up!

We're producing non-apostolic fathers, meaning we don't know how to impart into the next generation. We have young men who are gifted but no one checking him. We have charismatic bastards, with no fathers. You're making them by your absenteeism, the making of a manless society.

Stop telling your little boy how cute he is when they are twelve. Call him handsome. I heard some educated people saying that if their son wants to wear a dress, they'll let him. The Bible says, "Train up the child in the way they should go." Not the way they want to go, the way they should go. They need your help. You have an obligation. They don't have to be your son, just a son. I remember those days when I read that Scripture, it changed the game.

This is a burden for me.

I remember when I was a little boy, I was about five years, I used to suck my thumb. My mother would wear a silk slip, they don't wear those anymore because some women want everyone to see everything. So I would suck my thumb and put her silk slip between my thumb and index finger. It was my opium. So my mother bought me a blanket with a silk edge. My father lived three block away, never came over and provided no child support. He never did anything for us. But my uncle saw me and stepped in. He told my mom, "I don't want him dragging that blanket, sucking his thumb." So one day he saw my blanket and said, "Give me that blanket." He took my powder blue blanket, threw it in the garbage and made me watch it burn. I don't know if he was castigating me or castrating me but I was so angry. I could no longer suck my thumb nor have the sensation of sucking my thumb and feeling the blanket. I went up to him huffing and puffing and he hits me in the chest. The next time I saw my uncle I couldn't wait to get in his chest for him to come and pop me in the chest and say, "Thatta boy." When I was hanging with my mom I was sucking my thumb, but when a man spoke to my manhood, he called the man out of me. He was not my father, he was my uncle. God will bring someone in your life to show you you're not a pimp or a player, or a whoremonger, you're not a drug dealer but a world changer.

A few years ago, my wife was putting something in the dishwasher and the dishwasher was brand new because we replaced it. But it wasn't working and it would hold the water. My wife said we got to call the plumber. I said wait a minute, I am the plumber. I clean the pipes around here. I got offended. No muscle bound cat is going to come in here and fix my house. No. I am looking at the dishwasher and I pray, God you've got to show me what to do because I am the plumber. My wife went to bed, it was around midnight. I was on my other church, it's called YouTube. I learn all kinds of stuff on YouTube. All kind of handy stuff for the house. I searched "faulty dishwasher" and it showed me how to troubleshoot it. After three hours I came across this spot that said, "Generally when you replace your dishwasher even when the technician puts it in, there is a black plug that has to be knocked out with a hammer and a screwdriver. This is a plug most technicians do not remove. You usually don't notice until you've used the dishwasher five to ten times." I said, "Yes, that's it." It was about 3 in the morning by this time. I went in the back and got my hammer and screwdriver. I was getting ready to bust something up. I followed the YouTube tutorial, and sure enough there was a black plug which I proceeded to knock out. Then the dishwasher began functioning properly. I went upstairs and said to Pamela, my wife, "Hey, come down. You've got to see this. I fixed the dishwasher, I am the plumber and I have come to fix the pipes!"

Now let me show you what happened. See some people are ego deprived. Ego is the "i" in self. That's what you need to get up and go to work. You need ego, ego makes you wash your face. When you get out of bed, ego made you comb your hair. That's ego, because you care what you look like. You need ego. Ego made you pick out your clothes, match stuff and put on your perfume, sister. You got the matching watch with your blouse. Ego is not a bad thing. Ignorant people think it's a bad thing. But ego won't let you be disrespected. Ego won't let you be broke and satisfied. Ego won't let you settle for "that will do." Ego will say there's got to be more than this. This is not by destiny. I was created for more than this. Ego is what keeps you moving. It's the "i" in self. What happens to men in particular, according to the Wall Street Journal, African American women are the fastest growing prosperity group? Why are there more women with degrees than men? Why do men quit and not finish? You gotta check with your brother. For example, a man says he's gonna fix the screen. He painted it last year and didn't finish. Now the same paint doesn't even match because it's been sunburned, so the idea of him not finishing speaks to a core value.

So what's happening? Why are men being castrated? You may not like this but women are castrating men. Women are. You're dressing him, you're feeding him and then you're wanting him to be Hercules. You've got a big baby Huey. I recommend any young man that's getting married not move from their mother's house to marriage. Move from your mother's house to your house. To your apartment. That may be rough on you, but that's ok, it's supposed to be. Some people are paying their son's cell phone bill. They are are living in the house with a full time job. You're creating a castrated male.

As a homo-sapien you're supposed to know how to communicate, articulate, and use tools. Some men don't even know what a tool is. "Oh it's Phillip's screwdriver?" No it's called a phillips head screwdriver. He doesn't know what a screwdriver is. Bring me the monkey wrench. Bring me the crescent wrench. Bring me the channel locks. Crescent wrench? Come back with pliers? Is this what you are looking for? No. It's because his impartation has come from nurturing and not working. I have watched one of the famous Christmas movies, *A Christmas Story,* about a million times. Me my wife and children know all the lines. I remember the scene with the father and the son when they have a flat tire. He made his son get out and watch him change a flat. They got to watch you do something.

I was preaching in Kansas City one time. Now when a man walks up on you and you're sitting down, you are supposed to get up and shake his hand. I got to the platform and I am shaking everybody's hand and there is this man sitting down. I shake his hand and he doesn't move. It was just instinct, he didn't get up so I just yanked him up. It was just instinct. I said, "How you doing?" Then I walked away. I wasn't even thinking. I didn't even know the guy, but I wasn't going to let him disrespect me through his own ignorance. So I thought I would pull him into a place of education.

Now maybe I have offended some people with what I have written in this chapter. But offense shouldn't severe the relationship. Offence should not make you quit, it shouldn't make you throw in the towel, because you measure a man not by his offense, you measure a man by what he contributes to your life. And if the contribution to your life is greater than the offence you keep coming around, and keep reading.

Listen to me, the man who tells you to sow your oats is a crazy man. The man who tells you not to commit, is a crazy man. But listen to me, no offence to Stephen Curry or Lebron James, but those men are not your role models, they are called athletes. And guess what athletes do? They retire. But you never retire from manhood. You're going to have your DNA in you looking for a man to speak to your manhood. You can't help it. Something in you will call for it. I don't care how many women are in your life, you'll have this void in you. Something in you will cry out for it. I need a man in my life. I need a man to lay his hands on me. There is something succinctly different when a man brings impartation. Listen to me, your daughters are watching how you act men, because whether you like it or not, the man that you show them is the man that your daughters are going to be attracted to men. If you show them an irresponsible man who puts everything on the woman, no responsibility, there are going to be drawn to that type of trifle, no good man. I am watching these young women in church who are married and having a child. If your wife is pregnant you have a responsibility to make life easier for them. I have no regard for a man who has three or four children and his wife has to fight with him on the pew because he walks around like he has no responsibility. You are an irresponsible priest and a castrated man. There are some women today who have made up their mind, they don't want any of these men because they are watching how they do. But the time has come where we have to stop the making of a manless men. I am not talking about homosexuality, I am talking about castrated, psychologically castrated with no drive and no ambition. Your mother should not have to make you go to school, to get up, to clean up, to take a shower. Oh mom nothing. Let a man get a hold of you. I saw this little boy, about 9 or 10 here with his mother and grandmother raising him. He is sucking his thumb. And she says, I just don't know what to do with him. He is not even communicating at 10. I said, "Give me a week with him. "What are you going to do to him?," she asked. "It's not about what I am going to do with him, it's what you did to him."

This is a message for men. You've been castigated. When you're getting a beating and your mama says, "Just like your no good dad. You ain't nothing, you make me sick just like your no good father." Some people have cursed their father in the eyes of their son and if the father ever gets an epiphany and wants to come around their kids, they look at him like he's crazy cause you dogged him so bad.

Let's pray.

Father, I thank you that you are raising up men who are leaders, who follow you, who serve you and who lead our families and communities. Thank you for giving the women wisdom and guidance in raising the next generation of world changers and leaders. Help us follow you and raise up champions for Christ who will restore biblical manhood to our community and world. In Jesus' name, amen.

12 THE DANGER OF TWO RESIDENCES

Galatians 5:13-19, 13 For brethren, ye have been called unto liberty; only use not liberty for an occasion to the flesh, but by love serve one another.

14 For all the law is fulfilled in one word, even in this; Thou shalt love thy neighbour as thyself.

15 But if ye bite and devour one another, take heed that ye be not consumed one of another.

16 This I say then, Walk in the Spirit, and ye shall not fulfil the lust of the flesh.

17 For the flesh lusteth against the Spirit, and the Spirit against the flesh: and these are contrary the one to the other: so that ye cannot do the things that ye would.

18 But if ye be led of the Spirit, ye are not under the law.

There is a warning in this text. It gives us warning to be better men and women! I address in this chapter, the danger of living in two residences. I believe we are spirits, who have souls and live in bodies. I believe we live as one being, but have two existences. In other words I am the same man that lives in the spirit, but also lives in the world! Having two residences. Have you ever heard of a duplex? Maybe you live in one now. It's two separate entrances to live in the same building. That's a duplex. A flat uses the same door to get into multiple apartments, a complex has multiple entrances and exits, but you live in the same building.

You're the same person entering different buildings, and living in different places. We are in the Spirit, having access to two realms... Spiritual and natural! The concept of living duplicitously doesn't mean living in two places, but it often means living deceptively. Cheating yourself out of abundant life by thinking this life is all there is!

Yes, we're free, but don't use your liberty to be foolish. Now we're not under the bondage of the law, but be careful. Liberty doesn't function loosely!

So everything we do should be done through love. Whatever you do, do out of love. Don't do things only for people you love. Do everything out of love, it will balance your action's motives! Do everything because of love. When you try to choose people to do things for, based on the premise of anticipation, then you're not doing it for love alone you're doing it for reciprocity, to get something back. You're looking for a gratuity. Love is the locomotive of altruism - the unselfish concern for others. So whether they respond or not, give you credit or not, whether they appreciate it or not, it's inconsequential. Do it for love alone!

You may work a job that seems intolerable, but while you're there you should do the best you can! You should be there early and leave late, because you're doing it as unto the Lord! Even though you may not like your co-worker, or you may not like how things are done, do you best. You can still appreciate that God has given you this avenue, this venue to support your family, and bring income into your life! God said if you would be faithful over a few thing, He would make you ruler over many! This is for those who are chronically complaining about their job - you're cursing yourself! Before you got the job you were asking God to give it to you, but now you don't like it so much. Love is patient, love is kind, love covers a multitude of sin,. You can deal with a hard to get along with co worker because love covers a multitude of sin. Love alone let's you know. That coworker doesn't hold your destiny. You gotta be careful saying, "God I don't want to be here anymore." You're minimizing who you are! You don't know who you are in the kingdom. I have learned this experientially - God will keep some places operating just because you are there and you have a family to provide for. You need to know who you are in God! According to Romans Chapter 4, when you have the Abrahamic blessing on your life, God will make you a blessing. You're not only blessed, he will make you a blessing! Some people won't die prematurely because you are connected to them! Some people won't get into as much trouble because you are connected to them! Do you know a whole company can stay in existence because you are working there? You may say, "I never thought of it that way." You're the favor that feeds others, whether they recognize it or not!

The Bible says, "Walk in the Spirit and you will not fulfill the lust of the flesh." Walking is a lifestyle, fulfilling is an experience. He didn't say walking in the flesh, he said fulfilling the lust of the flesh.

So when the Bible talks about loving one another and not devouring one another, it says walk in the Spirit and you will not fulfill the lusts of the flesh. Again, you see walking is a lifestyle, fulfilling is an experience. You can go and do something and be fulfilled and have an experience and then move on. The flesh wants to be satisfied regardless of consequence, but walking in the Spirit is a lifestyle! Here's an example: you can go an spend $100 dollars on dinner for two, but you'll be hungry again tomorrow. The flesh is never really satisfied! Experiences are a web of facts and feelings. That is why you don't marry someone just because you don't want to fornicate. The flesh doesn't know faces! The flesh wants satisfaction, but not responsibility! That's why some people play house. They live together but are not married. Then you try and pray that God would bless your relationship, but He can't bless it because you are fulfilling the lusts of the flesh. The bed is defiled! The foundation is corrupt! You have a hip relationship instead of a head relationship.

You might disagree. You'd rather marry someone and not fornicate. The problem is when you marry someone you don't really love to keep you from sinning, your flesh doesn't recognize faces! This is why you see a man with a good wife, a beautiful wife, and he decides to cheat with a nasty, whorish person, no one can understand why he goes and does that. It's because flesh doesn't recognize faces and when it's satisfied with one, flesh will go to the other. It's never really being satisfied at all, because flesh in reality is never satisfied!

When a man is consumed with pornography, it's not because he's obsessed with sex, it's because he's obsessed with the release! They're release addicts! They aren't looking for relationships, just release!

When the Bible says, "Walk in the Spirit and not the flesh," there has to be more to your relationship than an orgasmic stimulation! Intimacy begins between the ears, in stimulating and intellectual conversation!

So what's happening is many people have divided their lives like you would slice a pie. They have "pied" their lives. They've compartmentalized their lives into a slice for their job, a slice for their life, family, church experience, God is a slice, money is a slice. The problem is it fragments you! But you can't pie God! He's got to be macrographed over everything! You need God in your money, you need God in your family, in your occupation. He needs to be over everything. God never wanted you to set your life up in separate slots. You have to deal with this. God never wanted secular and spiritual. Everything you do comes out of your spiritual man! How you balance your checkbook, how you do your job, how you raise your family. Everything you do! If you've got bad credit it ought to vex your spirit! If you've got delinquent bills you need to deal with it. But what happens many people are dancing but not developing! You can dance, but there is no walk in the Spirit! After you finish shouting you need to start walking! You'll get a check on how you deal with people. If I am walking in the Spirit, I am already convicted, I don't need you to catch me. When this thing is real, you'll feel bad before anyone catches you. You don't feel bad because you've been caught, you feel bad because you've been taught. When you walk in the Spirit, you'll get a check about how you are treating people!

Your flesh is contrary to the Spirit and has enmity with God, the Bible says.

Romans 7:19 says, "For the good that I would I do not: but the evil which I would not, that I do."

Romans 7:24 reads, "O wretched man that I am! who shall deliver me from the body of this death?"

The struggle is always on, and as long as you live you're going to struggle with this thing called the flesh. What happens is there are people who love God, but they treat church like it's optional! The church is God's conduit to meet us! This isn't laborious, this is for you to eat! Whenever you look at church as laborious, you've got the wrong perspective. When I come to church I feel better, not bitter. When I come to church I feel rejuvenated. When I come to church I get healing, I've learned that my inheritance is among those who are sanctified!

Anytime I am sick I am coming to the house of God, when I am low, I am coming to the house! When I'm up, I'm coming... David said my foot almost slipped when I saw the prosperity of the wicked, until I came to the house!

When you come to the house of worship, it's not about what you want it's what you need! He is not passing out pleasure principles, He's giving us nutrients for living! So sit down, sit back and say your grace. I have never come to church to support the service, I come to church because I'm hungry! Oh taste and see that the Lord is good!

Blessed are they which do hunger and thirst after righteousness: for they shall be filled. Matthew 5:6

The struggle is real, every day you have to deal with the crucible. Sometimes we call things blessings when it's actually stealing. You get change, you gave them $20, but they give you a $50. Integrity tells you that's wrong.

Don't retaliate, I want you to bless them. Blessed are the peacemakers. I am not doing it because you treat me right, I am doing it because I love God! Sometimes you've got to do things for love alone.

If the only reason you are attracted to someone is their physicality, that's a flesh hookup.

FAKED OUT BY THE FLESH!

Tamar was raped in the Bible by her half-brother Amnon, and then he hated her as much as he loved her. That's because he never really loved her, he wanted her flesh! Your pre Christ nature just wants the flesh. There are men and women who are in relationships that are supply and demand! That doesn't work in the kingdom, it has to be based on relationship, so when you know God, no is a wonderful answer. So when you ask God for things, it needs to be according to His will. You need to ask according to the will of God.

Adultery, fornication, witchcraft, emulations….these are works of the flesh! Those who do such things will not inherit the kingdom of God. So people are getting saved but are not developing as Christians! They are not committing to the word of God so that they know Him or experience Him. Therefore your lifestyle doesn't change. The reality is that when you walk in the Spirit you will not gratify the desires of flesh. When you're in the Spirit you know it's wrong. So what happens is you've got to spend time taking dominion over yourself. It's easy to tell other people what to do! Have you ever heard of someone say that they've got to get out of here, they can't do anything in this town, they've got to go the next town? The truth is the same person who is here is the same person who will be there! If you're jacked up here, you'll be jacked up there!

When you're entertaining, you're not singing praises. If I am entertaining, it's a flesh display! Many R&B singers aren't that great alone, some need props and lights. The flesh is going and you're looking at the flesh, so it becomes entertainment. Videos made some people famous when their voices couldn't because it's the image goes display versus their ability to sing! They'll pay you to entertain them, but they won't value you taking them to another level!

You can lust for power and still be dissatisfied. You don't need a significant other to be significant. You should be fine by yourself. You should be able to roll yourself. The flesh is always in disagreement to the Spirit of God. You've got to bring your flesh under subjection. People come to church to be delivered from the spirit of fornication, the spirit of homosexuality, but it's a work of the flesh. It's a behavior. You've got to bring your flesh under subjection.

The hard part is walking. When you can walk together, you have relationship. Walk this way. How you livin?

But then he said if you are led of the Spirit you are not under the law. You have to be Spirit led on your job. You have to be Spirit led dealing with you children. You can't say, you wanna be gansta. I'll give you a gangsta beating. You can't go street. In everything you've got to be Spirit led. Let me show you it works.

Proverbs 25:28 reads, "He that hath no rule over his own spirit is like a city that is broken down, and without walls."

In mathematics it's ok to say 2 + 2 is 4. But if you say "you is lying," that's bad English. Anytime you use the word "is" in math, you have to have two absolutely equal parts.

When a man says "I love you," he's got to be saying, "I *God* you." He can't say that he *Gods* you. You see, you can't give what you don't have.

125

So if you are not born again, you have to ask where did the origin of your love originate. Agapeo, you can't get that in your flesh. What kind of love do you have for me? Well I love you, you've got to be my woman. Beep. No.

Love demonstrated is demonstrative. You do stuff if you love someone.

When you demonstrate the love of God, you are going to have to start blessing people who hate you.

For if ye love them which love you, what reward have ye? do not even the publicans the same? Matthew 5:46

Start doing good to people who can't stand you, but need you. Then you're doing it for love alone.

But the reality is you don't have Christianity until you can love for love alone. I remember one time when I helped people out and they dogged me real bad. I saw the man who did this come into a restaurant with the suit I gave him, along with my shoes, and my tie that I gave him. I am sitting at a restaurant with my wife and he's walking like he doesn't even see me. It took the Holy Ghost to tie my tongue in a knot, then stand on my head because everything in me wanted to take that fork and fork him. I'm being honest. I wanted to stick him with the fork. What I am trying to say is I was just so offended. I paid his rent, I helped him when his car got repossessed. I blessed him and then he dogged me. If you're in the world that's a beat down right there. It took everything in me, the Holy Spirit, the Apostles, Jesus, everything that I could think of to keep me in my seat and to do good to someone who used me and despitefully mistreated me.

That was probably you one time too.

What we do is we disconnect our spiritual walk from everyday life challenges. We disconnect. So, "Praise the Lord" is only used in church. Then it's, "What up dog, hollar at you boy, holla at you. Look at the white shoes, look at the white shoes."

You're living in two realms, two residences.

I had to learn when I had nothing in my hand, I couldn't say God didn't provide because I was looking at the wrong hand. If I am living in the Spirit, I don't look at my hand, I look at the hand of God providing for me. When you pray, "Give us this day our daily bread," and it's night and you don't have it, when day comes you'll have it. God will provide it again. In the flesh you measure your whole life from one bad night. There's so many of us that say, "God I just don't know what I am going to do." Walk in the Spirit! So many people don't know what they are going to do because they are walking in the flesh. It's never predicated upon what's in your wallet or your purse. It's not dependent on your resources, it's dependent on God.

When day comes, God will provide for me again. So walk in the Spirit.

You may have cried about what you don't have saying, "God, I don't know what I am going to do." But there are some today whose trust is still in God. They can take your car, they can take your house, they can fire you off the job, they can repossess your TV, but what they can't take is your joy. Because the joy that you have, the world didn't give it to you! You need to tell someone, "I've got joy and the world can't take it from me." It's never predicated on what's in your purse, wallet, what you have or don't have or your history. It's for love alone.

John 3:16 says, "For God so loved the world, that he gave his only begotten Son, that whosoever believeth in him should not perish, but have everlasting life."

That word in Greek for so is *homeous,* which means he loved you so hard something happened.

God so loved the world that he gave his only begotten Son. Homeous. It means you love so hard that something manifests. If you say, "I love you," to someone, where is the manifestation?

Proverbs 25:28 says, "He that hath no rule over his own spirit is like a city broken down with no walls."

This is the same as having rule over your spirit. "Is" meaning equal to. When you don't have rule over your spirit anything can happen. Anyone can say anything to you and mess you up for the day. You let somebody get in your spirit. I can't control you but I can control what gets in here. You can act like a fool if you want to, but you'll act like a fool outside of my house. You won't step in my house and act like a fool, because in this house I control what goes on in here. You can say what you want to say, but I don't have to receive anything you say about me, I don't control you but I do control my spirit!

When you start walking in the Spirit and not fulfilling the lusts of the flesh, it's going to be hard for people to hurt your feelings like they used to. "She did me wrong," that's out on the outside, because the real change is on the inside. I have rule over my own spirit. You are not going to get in my spirit and get me upset. I didn't come to church to meet you anyway. I came to get a word from God. I am guarding my spirit from everything else that is not like God. You are not going to get in my spirit and get me upset. I am not at church looking for air condition, teleprompters, and padded pews. I'm looking for God! I am guarding my spirit from everything else that's not like God. Some people are taking medicine over someone else's funky attitude. Some people are having a nervous breakdown because someone else is acting like you've lost your mind! You aren't going to drive me to medication, I rule my own spirit. You ain't going to make me think I am crazy because all the hell I went through to get to this place in God! Then you're going to talk about my blessing, my favor, and try to make me feel bad? No way.

We need to walk in it. Walk in it. Walk in the Spirit and you will not gratify the desires of the flesh.

This is the danger of two residences.

You can't live in the Spirit and the secular. In two different realms. You have two existences, but one realm. I am a spiritual man. That's who got me in here. When I deal with you I've got to deal with the spiritual man. I gotta let him bring me in here, so I can be objective. When you start dealing with people and you're not spiritual, they're going to get in your feelings. I've shaken people's hands literally and I know they've talked about me. And I am shaking their hand and saying God bless you and that's not placation or being fake. I say, "Good to see you. Nice to see you. God bless you," and it's not placation, it's genuine. I have decided to not give you permission to get in my spirit and mess up my day. When you do that, people will call you arrogant, but I would rather be arrogant than irritated, because if I let you in, you're going to irritate me. "I can't believe he said that," you say. Believe it and get back to living! After a while when you don't respond to people's idiosyncratic behavior, they are going to think you're arrogant. No matter what happens in your life, you've got to keep living. I am not going to my job simply because I love it, I love what I am providing for! I am going for my babies and my family even when I don't feel like being there. I am not doing it for the thank you, I am doing it for the love alone!

God said he loved you before you were saved. He loved you first! If I love God and I am walking in the Spirit, everything about you is antithetical to the thing that I love. When you drop me off for church and pick me up from church, where are you in the middle during church? I am going to tell you the truth, you've got to walk in fellowship! Amos said, "How can two walk together unless they be agreed?" When I read the Scripture the conflict is complicated. You love God with all your heart, however the conflict asks are you fulfilling the flesh as you seek God for desires to be filled? Let me give you a flashback. I am talking about being saved and filled with the Holy Ghost right now. Experience is a web of facts and feelings. Depending on it, euphoria or dread is fulfilled. When you walk in the Spirit, it's a lifestyle. Fulfillment of the flesh is all about self satisfaction, that's why we stopped having prophets come to our church. They'd pack out the church because the people want to be satisfied, but we need celebrate the Savior! Many are not coming for God, they're coming because they want something from God!

I have been married for over 28 years and it seems like 28 years didn't even pass. I don't feel like it's been long dark days. One of the reasons for this is physicality played a minor role, but walking together became a major role! When you start growing with people, relationships go through a maturation process. This is when you start having covenant and enjoying the relationship. But it wasn't about the fulfillment of the flesh. It's about us, we, and our. It is based on plurality, and it's what we cover in premarital counseling. It's the same premise in the body of Christ - us, we and our. We don't just use the Gestalt Theory of Touch, the truth is you're better together than you are apart. We are by design emotionally expressive. You can't be me, mine, and I. Two, the Bible says in the book of Ecclesiastes, are better than one. That's not talking about marriage, it's talking about relationships. You've got my back, I've got your back. You may be you by yourself and feel that the walls are caving in, but when someone else is with you, you can trust and help one another.

Let's pray.

Father, thank you for the truth that two are better than one. You didn't create us to be alone, but to grow and prosper in a community of believers. Help us to support one another, challenge one another, and together go further than we could alone. In Jesus' name we pray. Amen.

13 THE POWER OF TWO

7 Then I returned, and I saw vanity under the sun.

8 There is one alone, and there is not a second; yea, he hath neither child nor brother: yet is there no end of all his labour; neither is his eye satisfied with riches; neither saith he, For whom do I labour, and bereave my soul of good? This is also vanity, yea, it is a sore travail.

9 Two are better than one; because they have a good reward for their labour.

10 For if they fall, the one will lift up his fellow: but woe to him that is alone when he falleth; for he hath not another to help him up.

11 Again, if two lie together, then they have heat: but how can one be warm alone?

12 And if one prevail against him, two shall withstand him; and a threefold cord is not quickly broken.

This is the power of two. Ecclesiastes was written by Solomon who was both the wisest and the richest man in the world. His point here is very poignant because with no ambiguity and no vagueness he says, "Two are better than one."

He also goes on to reemphasis that not only are two better than one, but that if you work with somebody your reward is greater than if you work by yourself and if you fall they are there to lift you up!

But he introduces us to this paradigm by telling us of a man who has no son, daughter or wife, who is all by himself. Solomon calls it vanity, there is no end to his labor, overtime, double time, no legacy, no posterity, he just works for himself and there is no one to enjoy or share it with. The society we live in values freedom and independence, but the society God is creating values interdependence, working together, and helping one another, altruism..

One day, Bishop O.T. Jones Sr., the former second assistant Presiding Bishop of the Church of God in Christ, and I were in the same town riding in a car together. He told me to learn the stories of the Bible. He also told me to study three things. He told me to study time, people, and history. He told me it would make you a man among men! When he said that many years ago, I took it to heart and I committed myself to study people, time, and history. When you look at people who have fallen in the world, whether athletes, CEO, or preachers, when they fall, many times they fell alone! I didn't say this, Solomon wrote it. He wrote, "Two are better than one." God didn't create you to be an island, he didn't create you to be alone. Sometimes you can tell by how people sit in church, they've gotten so acclimated to being their own counselor, their own help, thinking they don't need any external relationship. Can you imagine being by yourself, with no encouragement, and you just have to pull yourself out of it? That's not how it was meant to be. Trials are sometimes magnified because you are all alone, Solomon says.

You'd be surprised how many people don't grasp this. I am not talking about having a boyfriend or girlfriend either by the way. You need healthy relationships. You can know your future by your friends! Your connections determine who you are. If you have the same friends in your life you had when you were in 6th grade, and never added any new relationships to your life, you are not living the full capacity of this life. You're not experiencing God's best. Relationships are the currency of heaven. What God values over money and materials is relationships. When you are your own judge, counselor and encourager, you're going to drive yourself crazy! You're pouting saying, "No one likes me, no one wants to be around me," but are you willing to engage with people?

When you speak to some people it's almost a shocker sometimes. I am on a plane almost every week and people have to come past me and don't say anything. It's not that people are being bigoted or racist, it's just we have a tendency to be selfish. So I wait until they are almost past me on the plane and then right in their ear I say, "And how are you?" I don't want to talk the whole trip, but I do want to at least say hello and it changes the atmosphere! I believe the currency of Heaven is relationships!

Here's my point, accountability and support is critical. In order for you to have a productive life, you have to know without any apprehension that two are better than one. Some of you are hair cutters and bakers, manicures, and seamstresses and you're doing it out of your house. If you got together with each other and decided to get a building, the Bible says together the reward would be better. But some people are so selfish and self centered they can't think like that. You would have more increase!

The power of collusion is working together. It happens even in church. I've seen churches, and I've been all over this country and every continent except two, and I have seen churches literally right next to each other. With no regard for thinking that I don't need a church here because they are working in that vineyard. But even the guy who opens a bar doesn't open one right next door to the other guy. McDonald's doesn't let you open a franchise except it be a certain radius away from the other one. All franchises that they have from Subway to Curves to Pizza Hut will not let you open one without being a certain radius away from the other. But without regard to my brother or sister, we'll just open another church right next door because we are not thinking about working together, we're doing our own thing! Tim Horton's coffee shops won't let you open another franchise right next to another one. It helps keep the franchise successful. We don't purposely do things together often enough! You'd be surprised at the amount of people who've had a bad day, a bad month, and a bad year. Let me tell you something, those bad days, bad years, bad months that you had could have been shortened had you had people if your life. There is a propensity to go through life by yourself. Here's the Scripture that helps me deal with me and people relationships:

9 Two are better than one; because they have a good reward for their labour.

10 For if they fall, the one will lift up his fellow: but woe to him that is alone when he falleth; for he hath not another to help him up. Ecclesiastes 4:9-10

People will not work together in the church but they'll work together in the secular arena. They'll switch vacations, trade shifts, help one another, and be flexible. But in the church, no, it's, "I don't feel led." Next time, I am going to bring everyone a pencil so they can all "feel led." There are so many temperamental emotions that you can't get the job done and you look weak in your devotion to what you say you love!

The Bible says in the day of your adversity you faint, your strength is small. But you'll work with "atheist Bob." You'll work with gambling Susie, though she's playing the lottery and scratching numbers while you're at work. "God bless you Susie," you say. But to your brothers and sisters at church, you're not collaborative, you're suspicious. Let me hear you speak in tongues first. Let me check your spirit. What's your testimony? How long have you been at this church? Who's your family? Where do you get this hocus pocus, witch crafty disposition? You'd be surprised, I see it all the time.

So what happens in verse 10 is if they fall, one will lift up their fellow. You know why some people can't help other people? It's because they weren't in your life when you're walking, so you don't want them in your life when you're falling? If you're not walking with me and I fall, your hand is strange to me, so I don't know you when I fall. That's a strange hand because it wasn't in my life when you were up. Some people don't want a hand because they didn't have you in their life when they were up, so they don't trust the hand when they fall. But let me ask you this, can we fellowship before you fall? Nobody wants you in their life if you keep telling them what to do but there is no fellowship. Nobody wants advice alone.

That's why it's hard to have people in their lives. That's why they won't call anyone and then they get mad when no one reaches out. Can we fellowship before we fall? No one wants you in their life with all advice and no fellowship.

The large church functions in what is called a elephant paradigm. A smaller church functions in a mouse paradigm. The difference is a small church with 20, 25, 30 members, as soon as something happens, everyone is there fast! If someone is having surgery, they're in the parking lot with ice cream, cake, and flowers. All you did is make a phone call. If you want to have fellowship just go to the pastor's back yard. If there is a need in a small church, everyone gravitates toward the need, every one is there!

A large church moves slow, but when it gets there it knocks your socks off. If you're having surgery, you're one of 15 other people having surgery at the same time. Here comes the elephant. They didn't show up as quick as a small church, so it's easy to get upset. You're home and they weren't there for you. Yet when you'd tell them? Yesterday! Now you think the church doesn't care but you're hanging with an elephant. A mouse paradigm is quick, it's going to be little. One flower, one balloon. The big church, they may be slow, but when they get there, oh they're going to blow you away!

I had to marry the idea that not everyone wants to be a part of a large church, some folk want to be a part of a small church because they think a small church is more intimate, but that's not how it works. You just need to understand how it works. At our church, Zion Dominion Global Ministries, our drive is to have large church impact, but move like mice not a mouse. Our goal is to be as big as an elephant, but by mobilizing all of our members, we can still move quick.

What happens is if you've come from a small church to a large one, your moving from micro to macro. You can't have "your ministry," it's "the ministry," you have to connect with someone in the church to have placement. Ministry is finding a need and meeting it!

What happens when some people come to church? They think that what makes them affable in the church is that they have a personal relationship with the Pastor and First Lady. That doesn't work in a larger church. The pastors of a large church are called to be your spiritual leaders, not your spiritual buddies. We're called to proclaim the gospel and if you hang out here long enough, you'll find people to hang out with. I know that hurts, but I am not at my church to hang with everyone. If I spend all my time hanging with you, what about him? Then it'll be said that I have favorites! I'll tell you who my favorite is, it's my wife. She's the only one I kiss on the side!

See if your not careful you'll take offense to the idea that we don't have time for you, but that's not true. I have spiritual time for you, but my social time is for someone else. People take offense to that. If I take you to a larger ministry like TD Jakes or Joel Osteen, you won't even meet them. At our church we have a reception for first time visitors at the first and second service. Still people take offence. I understand what it is. It's because you are coming from a mouse paradigm. But if a mouse gets too close to an elephant, you know what will happen? Let me show you how this works.

If we have relationship and one of us falls, the Bible says, one will help up his fellow. The reason some of your trials and tribulations have been longer than they should have been is because you didn't have anybody in your life. I am not talking about cronies. I am not talking about people who are kissing up to you. I'm talking about people who love you, who are not impressed because of your accomplishments, but they respect you. Those are the kind of people when you're sitting in the house, feeling bad, they are there for you. Has anybody ever had a 'feeling' bad month, a 'feeling' bad week? Come on, can we be honest? Just because you've got your makeup on and your suit on at church, doesn't mean you didn't have a bad day or a bad month.

All of us have been through something, but I'm telling you, you went through too long because you didn't have anybody in your life! You need people in your life, because two are better than one. You need somebody who will come over to your house, ring your doorbell, yell through the windows, "I know you're in there! Answer the door!" Open up! Then they'll try the handle. "I know you're in there." They're banging on the door, trying the handle, not leaving until they find you. They're not leaving until you open the door!

"Oh my God," you think. They'll burst open the door, raise these windows up, make you take a shower, and get you out of that place! I'm taking you with me, those are the kinds of people you need in your life! They won't let you sulk in your self-pity, they will get you out of it and be with you during the good times and the bad times. They open your doors and they'll drag you out of there!

Those are the kind of people who will keep you from dying before time. Next thing you know you're in the car with your head hanging out like a puppy, happy to be out! Have you ever had someone come and get you when you didn't want to leave? Have you ever had someone come and pick you up when you didn't want to go anywhere? That was your therapy. You need people in your life who are not like you, but like you. It's worth repeating, you need people in your life who are not like you, but they like you. You don't have the same taste in food, you don't have the same taste in clothes, but you're cool like that. You need the kind of person who will admit you're depressed. You may be depressed. They're not going to sit there and be sad with you, they'll open the door and turn the lights on. They're not going to let you sit around the house and die while you're connected!

The Bible says two are better than one, when one falls, your fella will help you. That's the kind of people you want in your life. They'll put some money in your hand and won't tell anybody. Those kind of people, they know you are looking good, but you're broke as a she-hank. Just broke, looking good, but broke. You're so broke you left the o off in poor. It's just "po." P, o. Po. They won't tell anybody, they just tuck some money in your shirt. There is no announcement or fanfare. Those are the kind of people you need in your life. They'll hold you accountable. They'll say, "Look now, I gave you $300 now, don't forget your boy, don't forget your girl." You need those kind of people in your life. They want you to stand when life is trying to knock you over. There are enough people already hating on you. If I'm your boy or if that's your girl, don't let them put you in a box of dependency! Real people say something in effect, "Put your lipstick on, your false eyelash is falling off, come on get it together! I know you don't have anything but they ain't got to know!" They've got your back, and you need people who've got your back when you need your back covered. I don't need you to cover my back when I'm rolling, I need you to have my back when I'm falling. That's the power of two! The Bible says, "Love covers a multitude of sins." These are the kind of people who cover you when you're down, not expose you when you're hurting!

That's why fellowship is the currency of heaven. You've gotta have real, genuine relationship. It's gotta be intentional. Make it happen. Engage yourself. Some of the closest people in my life today, I would have never met if Jesus had not aligned every situation so we could get together. So you can think you don't need anybody. But I'm praying for you. You could be losing your mind and still think you don't need anybody, you do! You may be singing, "I am happy with Jesus alone. Happy with Jesus alone. You can have the whole wide world I am happy with Jesus alone."

Wrong song. It tells you you're without relationships, and all other pseudo (fake) statements of humility. I'm just a nobody trying to tell everybody about somebody who can save anybody. No, I ain't singing that! Who told you? Nobody!

I'm going to sing, "I pray for you, you pray for me. I love you. I need you to survive. I won't harm you with words from my mouth. I love you. I need you too. It is His will that every need be supplied. You are important to me. And I need you to survive." That's what I want to sing. If you pray for people and then gossip about them, it will make you hypocritical! Lord help us today. He goes on in verse 11,

11 Again, if two lie together, then they have heat: but how can one be warm alone?

12 And if one prevail against him, two shall withstand him; and a threefold cord is not quickly broken.

I remember when I was coming up we had people our school, bullies. You bully somebody today and it's a crime. They're calling the police, anti bully squad coming! Counselor at school. They didn't have that when I was coming up. When I was growing up they had no bully squad. Bullies were taking your lunch and your cookie! I had a peanut butter cookie with the pizza, and potato sticks, applesauce, and corn. Then the bully would come by, he had to be about 18 years old in the third grade. He'd come by and take your cookie, take your apple, a beautiful apple. The kind you polish up before you leave the house and put it in your bag. One day he took my apple. He was too big for me to do anything back, so I was trembling at the table. "What you going to do, what you going to do?" He was too big. I was trembling, trembling. All I did was shake and quake. I had some big friends though who could help me out. I'll tell you their names - Richard Roatan, they called him "Tons of fun," and Willie Greene. Willie Greene was just a kid but he would later become a bodyguard for Michael Jackson, Prince, and other celebrities!.

These are my childhood friends. And they were big. I didn't have to be big. I had some big friends!

One time that guy took my cookie, my peanut butter cookie with the fork imprints. I mean people would trade their whole pizza for a peanut butter cookie like that. People would trade anything for these cookies. But because I wasn't alone, I had friends with me, I got it back and he never messed with me again.

So today, I want to ask are you going it alone, or do you have people who you can count on when you're down, when you're in a tight place? Two are better than one!

Let's pray.

Father I thank you that you made us to be people of community. We are not supposed to be alone. It is not good for man to be alone, you said. Help us to open our hearts and connect with others, to think beyond ourselves, to lay down our pride and walk in the humility of Christ so that we can connect and help one another be all you made us to be for your glory. In Jesus's name I pray. Amen.

14 CONSIDER THE ANT

6 Go to the ant, thou sluggard; consider her ways, and be wise:

7 Which having no guide, overseer, or ruler,

8 Provideth her meat in the summer, and gathereth her food in the harvest. Proverbs 6:6-8

Women are provisional, men are promotional. Women are provisional, they have wombs, it's their nature to nurture. The ant has no ruler, no overseer, no guide, but they all work together and there is no bishop ant, no pastoral ant, no evangelist ant, they are all on the same level. The reason we basic intellectuals need leaders, teachers, and guides is because we won't work together by nature, so someone has to bring us together. An ant doesn't need a leader, they work together naturally.

148

You can take a piece of chalk, and draw it around your house. The ant will not cross that chalk line. You can see them gather, they all gather around the line. The ant knows it is some kind of powder and he is apprehensive to get it on his feet and bring it back to where he lives. He is apprehensive about getting it on his feet, and making a decision that would ruin the rest of his colony. He won't take a chance on bringing something home that could kill his future. So they will gather at the chalk line. How many of you will stop taking chances just to satisfy yourself. Consider the ant!

I had 3 or 5 ants get in the closet one time, but by the time my wife, Mrs. Hennings sees them, she'll say there are a thousand ants in the house! We needed some ant spray. So I got some spray, you would have thought the ant was about 3 feet tall because of all the commotion. I got some ant spray, I sprayed the spray and took care of it. It's not that they don't exist, they see the barrier of the spray and they don't make the sacrifice!

There was a hornet's nest once on the side of the house. You can not mess with a hornet's nest during the day, because they work while it's day. You gotta wait until night, when they all go back in the hive. So when night time came, I took the foam sprayer, sprayed the nest and then covered it with a bag. The spray doesn't kill them, it brings them into a state of comatose. The hornet doesn't have to be killed because it will die if you bring it into a state of immobilization!

Some creatures die when they can't go anywhere. If you ever see a mouse in a mouse trap that didn't catch him by the neck, it's still effective! It doesn't have to catch it by its neck. A mouse has to keep moving. So if its immobile, it will die. A mouse has a digestive track that cannot regurgitate. His metabolism says he has to keep moving or he'll die. Whatever he eats goes straight through him. A mouse can be trapped in a mouse trap by its tail and he'll be dead the next day, simply because he stopped from progressing.

When hornets fall asleep in a comatose state, they die automatically. I saw them start falling out of the hornet's nest with a lot of foam and a lot of hornets, I got nervous! Then I opened up the hornet's nest and they had these combs in there. Inside the comb there was a larvae. They had made it so once they seal it, they can't get in. But the larvae has to work its way out. They had actually designed it so that if they practice infanticide, which means eating your own offspring, they decided that they'll protect their future, even from themselves! If time got so hard that they had to start eating their own offspring, they can not even get to them because they made a barrier that will keep them from ruining their future, even if they lost their minds. Learn a lesson from the hornet!

Just about everything works together except humans. As smart as we are, we let something so idiosyncratic get between us and our neighbors and lose the greater accomplishment ahead. It drives me crazy to see people in the kingdom, choking over gnats and swallowing camels! It makes you just cringe when you hear people arguing over nothing. Well I just don't want to do this. I just want to send people back to the first grade. You know what this is called, "life!" Bees work together, pride of lions work together, even the ridiculous hyenas work together, but church folk can't master the power of two. Let me prove my argument. Acts Chapter 2,

And when the day of Pentecost was fully come, they were all with one accord in one place.

2 And suddenly there came a sound from heaven as of a rushing mighty wind, and it filled all the house where they were sitting.

3 And there appeared unto them cloven tongues like as of fire, and it sat upon each of them.

4 And they were all filled with the Holy Ghost, and began to speak with other tongues, as the Spirit gave them utterance.

See you're all here in one place, with one accord and in one place. Not just all together, but in one place. They got the same thing on their mind, in one place!

See you can be in the same place but not be in one accord. At my church for example, some folks are sleeping, some folks watching, some folks are playing video games. We're not with one accord, but we're in one place. If you can get these two things to kiss, having the same thing on your mind and being in the same room will birth a suddenly. The next verse says, "and suddenly." All you had to do, was have the same mindset just for a few minutes, in the same room, just for a few minutes. And God will give you a suddenly. Because He loves it when we use the language of unity like we, us, and our. When Joshua makes the statement, "As for me and my house, we will serve the Lord," he is touching on the concept of unity. Acts says, "And suddenly, there came a sound from heaven as of a rushing mighty wind." It is not a wind, it's a sound! There is no wind blowing, it's the sound of a rushing mighty wind. And the sound filled all the house, the Bible tells us. Why would God send a wind with your suddenly? I am glad you asked. First of all He wants to silence the conversations that are already going on! Sometimes you need the sound of the wind to silence the conversation! You can't be rude and silence the conversation so in order to get ready for your suddenly, God sends the sound of your suddenly to sanctify the atmosphere to get you ready for what's coming! The Bible says there sat upon each of them cloven tongues of fire. Cloven means split.

So when the Holy Ghost comes on them and sets on them like a fire, split, we are not connected but the Holy Ghost connects us and so when He splits/splinters, that brings you and I into fellowship. I don't have to know who's your mother, I don't have to know your daddy, I don't need to know where you were raised. All I need to know is what type of Ghost you got and if we got the same Holy Ghost, we got the same power. What kind of Holy Ghost you got?

Now watch, he sat upon each of them. Next verse, verse 4 says,

"And they were all filled with the Holy Ghost, and began to speak with other tongues, as the Spirit gave them utterance.

5 And there were dwelling at Jerusalem Jews, devout men, out of every nation under heaven.

6 Now when this was noised abroad, the multitude came together, and were confounded, because that every man heard them speak in his own language.

8 And how hear we every man in our own tongue, wherein we were born?

9 Parthians, and Medes, and Elamites, and the dwellers in Mesopotamia, and in Judaea, and Cappadocia, in Pontus, and Asia,

10 Phrygia, and Pamphylia, in Egypt, and in the parts of Libya about Cyrene, and strangers of Rome, Jews and proselytes,

11 Cretes and Arabians, we do hear them speak in our tongues the wonderful works of God."

Speak the language of your era!

153

People are confounded because you can understand each other. Now you should have been confounded because we are not speaking. That should confound you that we are not talking to each other. But you're not confounded that we are not talking, you are confounded that we are talking. And the Bible tells us that when the Holy Spirit comes upon us, they began to speak in other tongues. Every man heard them speak in their own languages, when you are really in unity, you understand my language. When the Holy Spirit comes in you learn how to hear me.

I don't want to be around people who just want to be heard, but don't want to hear me. You don't have to know what happened to me but if you've got the Holy Ghost you can hear my pain. You know when I'm struggling, because you are connected by the Spirit of the living God. I don't want to be around people in church, that say, "Where is Johnny?" "I don't know, nobody's seen him. If you've got the Holy Ghost as the Scriptures says, it allows you to hear every man.

Can you hear me now?

Because when the Spirit of God comes, you can hear me, you can see me. Something in your spirit says, go check on Roderick, something in your spirit says go check on Susie, something in your spirit says go check on Pam.

You say, "I didn't call them, I checked on them through Facebook, and couldn't get in touch." Some things are spiritually discerned. If we have unity, we learn to speak to each other. The Bible says every man heard them in their own language. I understand your language now. I can hear where you are. Don't give me that fake pseudo Christianity, that you don't have time for me. You ain't seen me, or thought about me.

But when it's real, something in my spirit says let me check on my brother, let me check on my sister. That's real relationship. And they were confused that we can actually hear one another. I don't have to have your ethnicity; I don't have to be black, white, or hispanic. I don't have to be rich or poor, all we have to have is the same Spirit. And if we've got the same Spirit, you can hear me and I can hear you! Jesus Christ, when He sent out the disciples, He sent them out two by two. The men who went out by themselves left God. Read it, you want to know who? Judas. Nobody was with him. Thomas did not receive the Holy Spirit because he wasn't there when Jesus breathed on them, he was by himself! There is a danger to doing some things by yourself! Jesus sends them out two by two. And they did things great in the kingdom. But you've got to get passed your own egomaniacal disposition and you've got to understand the Bible is polyglottal. Polyglotism is a collaboration different languages and writing styles. It goes in different kinds of understanding. It's mixed. You've got to know when God is talking to you, you've got to know when to be quiet. You've got to know peace and then let God guide you. When Paul is in jail, nothing is said of him doing anything miraculous, but when he got put in jail with Silas, two are better than one. But when you've got somebody to encourage you and say while you're in prison let's sing, "Come on wake up man, wake up girl, while we in prison we might as well give God glory." The Bible says Paul and Silas sang praises and praised God in the jail cell. The Bible says when two or three gather together in my Name, I'll be in the midst. God wants you to be with somebody.

All of a sudden while they were singing praises, the Bible says an earthquake came, and the gates of the prison opened on their own accord, chains popped off, and they never asked God to deliver them, or God get me out of here, all they did was sing praises, praises will open your prison doors, praises will break the chains off of your life, you need somebody to praise God with. Will you praise God with me?

You better start asking your friends, "I know we're cool, I know you're my boy, but can you praise God? I know you're my girl, but can you praise? I know you can fight but can you praise? I know you can cuss but can you praise? I know you can tell folk off, but can you praise? Because when my prison time comes, I don't need a fighter, I don't need a complainer, I don't need a liar, I need a praiser!" That's called a suddenly!

Acts chapter 3, Peter and John went to pray at the time of prayer, there was a man lying at the gate called Beautiful. There is a man lying there who asks for help, Peter replies, "Silver and gold have we none, but what we have we give to you, in the name of Jesus Christ, rise up and walk."

Peter takes him by the hand and he starts walking around. Now I am convinced, it would not have happened if Peter had went by himself. But Jesus said, "When two or three are gathered together in my Name," not two or three playing poker, not two or three playing spades, but when two or three are gathered together in my Name! I'll show up and give you a suddenly, I'll show up and give you a miracle, I'll show up and open a door that you didn't know existed! Get ready for your suddenly. Get ready. That means we've got to agree, that means we've got to pray, it means we've got to trust each other, it means we've got to think good of each other, it means we've got to endorse one another! Get ready for your suddenly.

Speak life. Get past idiosyncrasies. Get past mundane things that don't mean anything, get past the inconsequential, get to the real issues! We have some demons to conquer, some devils to whip. We've got some battles to fight. We've got some real issues to deal with.

You need some people in your life that don't necessarily shop with you, get manicures, with you, or golf with you. You need some spiritual people that you only call when intercession and prayer is needed! People who you talk with when are going through things...and pray together. God has some people in your life who are that part of your life.

Your promotion is tied to somebody in your life who you don't even want to be around. You need to learn how to engage. You gotta make it intentional, that's why we need overseers, rulers, guides, because we won't by nature engage each other. Sometimes it's a psychological problem. The hour has come for our relationships to be more than these pseudo, superficial, fake, "God bless you" relationships. I can't give you my hand when I fall if I can't trust you when I am walking. That's for all the people who want to tell you what to do but don't know how to fellowship.

Communion is not prayer, it's breaking bread and communication. The Greeks called it *koinonia*. The truth of the matter is two are better than one. The church is the Bride, Jesus is the Bridegroom, it's a wedding, two are becoming one. He prayed, "Father, make them one as we are one." Jesus said when you see me, you've seen the Father. Can you imagine getting that close to God? When you have relationships in the body, you go further. Jesus died that none would perish. The Scripture says whosoever believes shall be saved, he who doesn't shall be damned! I'm glad somebody brought me to church. I've met some people who I would have never known had I not given my life to the Lord! I am thankful for that.

Let's pray.

Father, thank you for the unity and fellowship within the body of Christ. Thank you that you called us to do life together, to do ministry together. Thank you that we are learning how to walk and fellowship in unity, to not just be in the same room together but to be in one accord.

15 WHAT DOES THE RESURRECTION MEAN?

Luke 20:34 And Jesus answering said unto them, The children of this world marry, and are given in marriage:

35 But they which shall be accounted worthy to obtain that world, and the resurrection from the dead, neither marry, nor are given in marriage:

36 Neither can they die any more: for they are equal unto the angels; and are the children of God, being the children of the resurrection.

For some unknown reason, we have really underestimated the power of the resurrection. Now I don't want you to get it confused, just because you got up doesn't mean it was a resurrection. Sometimes your get up is your comeback. There's a significant difference between a comeback and a resurrection! According to the Scripture, once there is a resurrection, you never die. If you're the children of the resurrection, you never die. Death to the saint is not annihilation, it's separation! Death becomes a vehicle for you to move from time into eternity. Preceding verse 34, you'll see the question was posed by the Sadducees, where they ask what if a man is married to his wife and he dies, and then she marries his brother. According to Levitical law, you'd marry your brother's wife, and have children in the dead brother's name. That was the law of Leviticus. That's why God killed Onan because he was supposed to have children in his dead brother's name however, when he went into his brother's wife after he died, he spilled his seed on the ground. And God killed him because he wasn't supposed to abort that which was supposed to be the future. That's another chapter. Now when you get back here, he asks what if he dies, and he marries her, and her other brother, that's three men, then four men, then it gets up to approximately 6 or 7 and then the question is when she gets to heaven, whose wife will she be? Who will be her husband? Jesus' comeback is there is no marriage and neither are men given in marriage in heaven!

So when you open a newspaper, and I know it looks nice, and it says, "Back together again," when the husband and wife die, but they aren't back together again because there is no marriage. See if you had the cares of this life superimposed onto your spiritual man. Then you couldn't enjoy heaven when you had a son who hadn't given his life to the Lord. You couldn't walk around heaven thinking about your grandmother, thinking about your sister, thinking about your grandfather, who didn't give their lives to the Lord, you wouldn't enjoy heaven with the cares of life on your mind. So when you step into eternity the cares of this life are over. You're not given in marriage neither can you be married, matter of fact marriage was for time living on this earth. It was a microcosm of what God has with His church. But when you get to heaven, I know you can't fathom it now, but let me walk with you through the Bible. When my wife and I get to heaven, we won't be there as Mr. and Mrs. Hennings, as a matter of fact, according to the Scripture, I won't know her as my wife. That's profound because the whole concept, the whole theology of marriage is for you being in time. That's why I don't know how you can waste time in this life when you only have the time God gave you. Because once this is up you can never come back to this again. That's why I am saying it again that you've got to learn how to forgive fast, laugh out loud, and love hard. Am I talking to anybody? Forgive fast, laugh out loud and love hard.

You've only got the time allotted that you can enjoy while you are here. So Jesus then goes on to say that in heaven there is neither marriage nor one given into marriage, as the children of the resurrection you never die. Someone in my congregation told me that she just buried her mother a few days before. It just lifted something off her to know that her mother did not die, the way we say people die, but Jesus said if you're children of the resurrection you don't die, you transition. So when you get this glorified body, there will be no artificial hip, no titanium hip, lasek surgery has nothing to do with glory. Dentures, hair weaves, front laced eyebrows, raised blade eyebrows, acrylic nails, none of that is going to be needed because the glorified body you get can not even be compared to what you left behind. Thank you Jesus.

I am so excited to know that trouble doesn't last always. And the fact that we are children of the resurrection, Paul said for me to die is to gain. Because if I leave here knowing him, we'll be sad, we'll grieve, we'll mourn, but we're stepping out of the corruptible and putting on the incorruptible!

Let's go a little deeper theologically. When you go to the book of Genesis, you'll find out that the Bible says Adam and Eve were naked and not ashamed. Now how can you be naked and not be ashamed?

First of all just because our ideology is so finite, based upon Western culture, we think when someone is naked they are being exposed. But they were naked and not ashamed before sin came on the scene, which meant they didn't have any garment. We don't need a garment if we have no shame. They were clothed in the glory of God. How do you know? Genesis chapter 3 tells us when they ate of the forbidden fruit their eyes were opened and they knew they were naked. Genesis chapter 2 says they were naked and not ashamed which meant I was naked but I didn't see you as being naked in the sense of being exposed, I see you as having been glorified. When you are dressed in the glory of God, a Tom Ford suit can't hang, St. John can't hang, Iskota can't hang, Versace, Gucci can't hang. Christian Louboutin can't touch what you look like when you're dressed in glory!

So now that I am living in this life I am going to take off this man suit and step in the glory on my resurrection day. I am getting light for the flight. So no matter what you do to this body, it's going to decay, its imminent, it's going to happen, but Jesus said we are children of the resurrection. What is resurrection? I am glad you asked, it's from the Greek word, not the english word resurrection. The Greek word *anastasis*. Anastasis means to rise up past death. So when you are resurrected, you come out of death. Healing is not resurrection, you can get a miracle of healing and still die. But healing is not resurrection. Once you have resurrection, the Bible says you shall never die.

Let's go a little further, now not only is Jesus bringing resurrection,

Jesus said I am the resurrection. You can be a secular humanist, you can be a Islamist, you can practice Mohammedanism, Buddhism, Hinduism, out of all these religions, none of them espouses resurrection. Jesus the Christ says not only do I resurrect, I am the Resurrection. I know we watch a lot of talk shows and they tell you this, that and the other, and that there are many ways to get to heaven. Janelle Monae says if your religion speaks against homosexuality and lesbianism you need to find a new religion. Wrong! There is no new religion. Jesus said I am the way, the truth, and the life, no man cometh to the Father, except by Me!

Some people name their daughters Anastasia, it actually means to rise up pass death. Which means you break some rules and some laws. In the book of St. John chapter 11, there is a story of a man named Lazarus who had two sisters, Martha and Mary. Lazarus was sick and in need of the Savior. Jesus was on his way coming from Judea and he told his disciples that he was going towards where Mary and Lazarus were. Thomas says, "Let us go with him also that we may die with him." He thought they would be stoned going there, but when he was on his way he stopped for two days. Then the Bible says when he arrived, they said, "Jesus had you have gotten here, our brother would not have died." Jesus responded, "Your brother is not dead, he will not die, he is alive." Martha said, "I know we'll see him in the resurrection." Jesus responded with great authority and said, "I am the Resurrection!"

Luke says He is the God of the living and not the dead, you can think that you're dead but the fact that Jesus shows up means there is life left! Because He's not showing up for dead things! And if things look dead and He shows up and He says, "I am the resurrection, you're worth bringing back to life." By the time he got there, the Bible says, they said had you been here, our brother would not have died. The Bible says, behold how he loved him because he wept. He cried. The Bible says Jesus wept.

He says to the crowd, this is in the text, "roll away the stone." Now why does he need them to roll away the stone if he is going to perform a resurrection? Lazarus should be able to walk right through like a ghost. But when you are resurrected you still have a physical body, you're not a spirit, you just have a brand new body with no blood. Jesus appeared after he was crucified, he came to the disciples and said, "I am not spirit, I have flesh and bones." We don't say flesh and bone, we say flesh and blood. But he says flesh and bone because there was no blood in his new body because it had already been shed that we might be saved.

He then says, "Roll away the stone." He wants the same people who blocked him to move the block out of the way. He tells the people, "Roll away the stone." So they roll away the stone and he calls Lazarus. "Lazarus, come forth." He comes up out of 55 steps below sea level and he's been mummified. How do you know? I've been to Israel. I saw the grave, I saw the cave. They don't bury them 6 feet deep. They put them in the back of a cave. He had to call Lazarus by name, because had he said 'come forth' a whole lot of folks would have been coming out. Aren't you glad he knows your name? Lazarus comes out and he is mummified, they had no intention of him being free. He is so mummified that they wrapped his legs, his thighs, his upper torso, his face, his mouth. But he hops on up out of there, because Jesus called him out. I don't care what's holding you back, if he calls you, you gotta come up out. If he calls you, you gotta come out. There are some people in our church who are married with children and were addicted to crack, you gave your testimony. They never went to AA or Narcotics Anonymous and they heard Jesus call their name and right there on the altar they were set free. Jesus took it right out of their system, took the smoke out of their lungs and showed them who they really were. He says, though you were dead, yet shall you live.

You may not have been addicted to crack, but something had a hold of your life. And when nothing else could help, love lifted you. Let me give you the reason why Americans are apprehensive about our children's future. The meaning of Lazarus is without help.

Can you imagine that God brings deliverance to you and make ways for you, and folks won't celebrate and give God glory and honor, because of what happened for you? I'll tell you why. There are folks in church right now, they don't like you, but need you! And they gotta bite their lip, their sitting next to you, and they know without you they won't get to the next level. God can give you a Lazarus miracle! What is a Lazarus miracle? When God does it without help! When he does it without assistance. When He does it without employing anyone else!

That's why some folk can't figure out how you got blessed and they didn't have their hand in it. But I am thanking God for the Lazarus miracle. He did it without help. He saved you without help. He brought you out without help. And once you've had resurrection there is no more death. When he comes up out of the grave, Jesus says to them, "Loose him and let him go." Now he told the people to move away the stone, and then take off that grave suit. It does not say give him a new set of clothes. He said take off what you put on him, because in his glorified state there is nothing he can wear, that can match how he looks!

In John 12, Lazarus is in the house having dinner. After resurrection there is no more death. Some people are rebarbative. When you are rebarbative you are a person who causes irritation, when you're rebarbative you cause aggravation. Those are the kind of people who when God does something for you, you are so excited, He made a way for us, He did it, and some will say, "Yeah but you've got to be careful." They are rebarbative and you can't have rebarbative people around you when you are trying to move in God!

Some people don't think it takes all that, but they don't know where you are trying to go. Some people will be in this same spot next year, but for some reason they are in the same spot but you look further away. You know why? You moved and they didn't! Rebarbaratin is when people are causing aggravation and irritation. I am believing God for this, trusting God for this. They'll say, "Yeah but I don't know, I just don't know." It's not about what you know, it's about what I believe. When Lazarus does come out, he doesn't get a new set of clothes, but he's having dinner.

In the Bible there was a woman, a young girl who is about 12 years old- the daughter of Jairus. The message is sent to Jesus that Jairus's daughter lies dying, the book of Matthew says. Luke says, "She's dead." And now we have the situation of dying but not dead. That's why you've got to have the right person telling you information! The message gets to Jesus and he is on his way Jairus's house. He says if you will just come and lay your hand on my daughter, because she lays dying. But on his way to Jairus's house he is moving through a crowd of people and there is a woman with an issue of blood who is pushing through to touch him. Now the woman with the issue of blood thinks if I can just touch the hem of his garment, I will be healed. See you don't get excited because you are thinking of the hem and the seam of a dress, but the priest had a long robe and when the priest would walk with the robe, they would pick up the robe and throw it over their shoulder between their shoulder blades. So when the priest would walk, the hem would be up around his back. Now the Bible says in Psalm 133,

"Behold, how good and how pleasant it is for brethren to dwell together in unity! It is like the precious ointment upon the head, that ran down upon the beard, even Aaron's beard: that went down to the skirts of his garments;"

If you did the study you would know that the priest's robe had a cuff equivalent to the cuff in my pants. So when the oil came, the oil ran down Aaron's head, down his beard, into his garments so his cuff is filled with oil. Then he takes the robe, slings it over his shoulder and there is oil in the air. The woman with an issue from a distance sees the priest and she sees the oil in the air and she think, if I can just touch the hem, I will be made whole. Not the seam by his feet, but between his shoulder blades and she tried to sneak a healing and touch him and her blood dried up. The disciples said, "How can you worry about who touched you with all these people around?" He said, "who touched me?" I felt power, virtue, and authority leave me." What do you mean who touched you, look at all these people?" There can be a lot of people in the room but only one gets to touch him. He said, "I felt power leave" and her blood dried up. In the meantime, he's walking now to the house of Jairus and when he gets there they told them she was dead. But Jesus said, "I am. I am the Resurrection. I'm more than a healer. She got a healing by accident but this girl is getting a resurrection on purpose."

When He gets to the house He asks them, "Do you believe?" He says, "Yes I believe, because nothing is impossible to them that believe." The Bible says he took Jairus's daughter by the hand and he said, "Arise, damsel. Arise." And the girl got up. And when she got up that's resurrection because by the time he got there she was dead. How do you know? Because on the way to her house he had healing in reserve but the bloody woman took the healing by accident and he says all I got left is resurrection power to get to this next house.

I'm so glad that when He's late, He's better. Thank God that when He's late, He's better. You're trying to rush God and make him hurry up. No, no, when He's late, He's better. That girl gets up, read the text, she never dies again.

In the book of Ezekiel there was a valley full of dead men's bones. You know you are dead when there is no tissues, no sinews, muscles or flesh. The bones are bleached white from the sun, crows and vultures have plucked all the flesh off of it. Past fagapotosis, past that point of flesh rotting away. There is no life there. Or is it? The prophet said, "Lord can these bones live?" God said, "Prophesy to the bones."

Jesus said in St. John chapter 1 in the beginning was the Word, and the Word was with God and the Word was God. So when he prophesies here he is giving them bones, them bones, them hambones, resurrection power. How do you know? Because they're dead. Preach to the bones. Why would God preach to dead bones in a dead place? Because he can see life in places that you and I don't see. Don't give up yet. Don't give up on your sons and daughters, your husband or your wife.

The Bible says he prophesied to the bones and three verses later the bones came together and the bones started realigning. Just from the word. The sternum got back together. The spinal cord got back in place. The rotator cuff got back into place. All the different parts of the body, the clavicle got back in place, knee joints, and then the bones stood up. How can you just sit there like the chosen frozen? How can the bones stand up and there is no brain, no heart, no lungs, no right and left aortic valve, no ventricle, no kidney, no spleen, no liver, no intestine small or large, there's nothing inside based on organs. All the bones have is a word. There is a skeleton standing up giving God praise with no larynx, giving God praise with no esophagus, bones are giving him glory. And here we are all wrapped in flesh, lipsticks, lashes, suits and beards, and won't open our lips and give God glory. And here are bones with no lips and no mouths and no tongue still giving him praise because when he gives you resurrection power you can do what you could never do before. How do you know? Because the Bible says, "Greater is he in me that is in the world." In the Name of Jesus by the authority of God he has put resurrection power in you. This means you will not die before time, you will not end your life circumstanitsciensciouly, you will not actually abort your future, because you've got some resurrection power in you, reserving you for what you've got coming. Cry, but live. Pout but live. Walk the floor but live. Lose some sleep but live. Fast but live. Sleep in but live. Do what you got to do but live. Because if resurrection is in you, you never die. Live! Live! Live!

Don't get it twisted, you can not have resurrection without Jesus. You can not have abundant life without Jesus. Are you hearing me? You can't have resurrection without Jesus. You can go to church all you want, but you better have Jesus. Young and old alike. What does a resurrection mean? It means life past death. There is a getting up day. You are going to put off the corruptible and put on the incorruptible.

Some people ask how can you preach on heaven and you've never been there? Some preacher on social media said he quit pastoring because the Bible isn't real, because God isn't real. He said this on social media. Let me tell you something, in the book of John, Jesus asks, "What do you think of the Christ?" He says this to the Pharisees, and they said, "You're the son of David." Jesus says, "If I am the son of David, why does David call me Lord?" He said, "Before Abraham was, I AM." And because they could not answer him, the Scripture says they asked him not another question. I will not spend the rest of my life trying to convince people that God is real. We walk by faith and not by sight.

God has no theogony, the origin of a god. I know where Molech began. I know where the Indian god started for the Hindus. I saw the big Buddha. They all have origins, but in the beginning, God!

Don't underestimate the power of Jesus Christ. He said, "I am the resurrection and the life." He is more than a healer. To prove my argument he resurrected Lazarus and the next week Lazarus is in the house having dinner in a resurrected body! Thank you Jesus! When you have a resurrected body you aren't just a spirit. When you die you don't go directly to heaven if you're a believer. You enter into the "rest" of God. If you aren't saved you go to hell immediately. There is no purgatory, to all my Catholic brothers and sisters. There is no rest for the wicked, according to the Scripture. If you're lost, how will you know? You'll know. When you die and there's no rest, you'll know! Why all this fire and brimstone, people ask if God is a God of love. Why is He sending people to hell? He didn't send people to hell, you sent yourself. How? By what you didn't do, you didn't accept, repent, and believe! When you died as a believer, you go to sleep, and rest if you know Him. The Bible emphasizes we will enter His rest. Don't be afraid, you're not going to be sleeping in a coffin! During rapture, the dead in Christ will arise with a new body and those that remain will be changed in a moment, in the twinkling of an eye. That's the Bible. Hell is real. There is a part of hell where you just keep falling. John says there is a resurrection of damnation if you don't know God and a resurrection of life if you know Him. So there is a body that is designed to be tormented forever. I am not cursing but I am saying it in advance, "Hell no I don't want to go!" I don't want to visit, I don't want to go on a field trip! I don't get these people who say they died and I visited hell. No, I don't even want to see pictures....No I don't want any part with hell! They say we'll send you a t-shirt, no I don't want a t-shirt that says "I've been to hell" no I don't want that.

Hell is so real that the Scripture says hell has enlarged its borders, it's getting more people than expected. Heaven is not enlarging its borders, but hell is enlarging its borders. What does a resurrection mean? Life passed death.

Let's pray.

Father, thank you for the resurrection of Jesus. Thank you that you defeated death, hell, and the grave. Thank you that you rule over all things. Thank you that when we believe we will see the glory of God and meet you face to face for eternity. In Jesus' name, amen.

16 Feel the Fear and Do It Anyway

Judges chapter 6 says,

13 And Gideon said unto him, Oh my Lord, if the Lord be with us, why then is all this befallen us? and where be all his miracles which our fathers told us of, saying, Did not the Lord bring us up from Egypt? but now the Lord hath forsaken us, and delivered us into the hands of the Midianites.

14 And the Lord looked upon him, and said, Go in this thy might, and thou shalt save Israel from the hand of the Midianites: have not I sent thee?

15 And he said unto him, Oh my Lord, wherewith shall I save Israel? behold, my family is poor in Manasseh, and I am the least in my father's house.

16 And the Lord said unto him, Surely I will be with thee, and thou shalt smite the Midianites as one man.

17 And he said unto him, If now I have found grace in thy sight, then shew me a sign that thou talkest with me.

18 Depart not hence, I pray thee, until I come unto thee, and bring forth my present, and set it before thee. And he said, I will tarry until thou come again.

Feel the fear and do it anyway. One of the main components or constructs that causes depression is fear. Most of the time when people struggle with fear, they struggle with fear based on the premise of what they project in their thought life. They don't even know for certainty what's going to happen; it's your negative anticipation of what you think is going to happen. Consequently it throws you into trepidation and anxiety, and it can drive you insane.

According to the American Medical Society, the number one problem that leads to depression is fear. And some people will never start their business, they'll never start their job, they'll never make that invention, because of the anxiety of what if it doesn't work? What if I lose money behind it? I don't want to lose my 401k. We'll go through all kinds of excuses because fear grabs you by the throat and chokes the potential right out of you.

This is the same situation that happens with Gideon. By the time you look at Gideon, in chapter 6 in Judges, he is the fifth judge in Israel and

IT'S A MATTER OF DOMINION

the son of Joaz. When he comes on the scene, God calls him and he has an acute inferiority complex, and he says three times, "Oh my Lord, oh my Lord, oh my Lord, not me, not me, I know you couldn't be using me. I am the least of my family, we live in Manasseh, we're poor, I know you don't have plans of using me." Because of his inferiority complex, God tells him, "I am using you, you are going to be the mighty man. I am going to destroy the Midianites, and you are going to do it as if you were one man." So Gideon asks for a sign next. He's got to know that God plans on using him. God gives him a sign, the Scripture says, "God says, I will tarry until you come again." You should have just shouted when you read that. Because if God has a plan for your life that is strictly, succinctly, distinctively designed for you, to the point where he will wait for you to come back, then he must really have made an investment in you. God tells Gideon, "I will tarry until you come again." He said I am going to wait on you until you get yourself together. Now I know in Pentecostal circles, as soon as you slip, they'll put you in hell. In Pentecostal circles, you can't mess up. But according to the the Scripture, God is into comebacks. God says, "I will tarry, I will wait until you come back. I'll wait until you come again."

Let me prove to you that God is into comebacks. You remember it was Lot who was in the land of Sodom and Gomorrah, and God was about to destroy it with fire and the Bible says Lot lingered. While he lingered, God waited, God did not let the fire of judgement hit Sodom and Gomorrah, until Lot got out of there. God waited on him. There was a

177

certain man who had two sons. One asked for his inheritance and left home. He then fell on hard times, sold himself to another citizens, and couldn't even enjoy the pig's food. He was a Jewish boy, and he was in the pigs pen. He finally came to his senses and said to himself, how much food does my father have to spare and I am here perishing with hunger? The Bible says he came to himself and went back to his father. The Bible says the father saw him from afar and ran to his son, and fell on his neck and kissed him and said, this is my son who was lost and now is found. God is into comebacks, let me prove it to you.

Here you are today in the will of God but nobody reminded you that before you got saved that God had his hand on you, because what you were doing, other people were doing and they are dead or in jail, but you didn't die! You're not in jail, you're reading this now, you're where you are today, and that fact gives us presupposition that God has waited on us! Some people did the same things you did and they are not here today! You better stop telling people you're going to reap what you sow, because a whole lot of people have sown many detestable things, and we are not reaping everything we have sown! Thank God!

Because God waited on you to get yourself together. Don't you let me impute on you a personal conviction. Just because I am not running as fast as you that doesn't mean I don't have it together. God will wait on you until you get yourself together. You don't believe it? He is called the God of all grace. What is grace? Time. Time to get it together. Time to repent. Time to do it over the right way. Time to say you're sorry.

Time to make it right. Grace gives you time! There is no one who can make a man feel bad about restoration, because if God didn't want you here, you wouldn't be here today. Yeah, but I know what you've done, yeah so does God, and yet He says I will tarry until you come again. He will wait for you to get yourself together. He tells Gideon He will wait on you. Then Gideon says I am going to bring a present. He brings a sacrifice of cakes. The angel of God takes the cakes off the rocks, with fire God comes and receives it. Then Gideon builds an altar and names it Jehovah Shalom, which means God is my peace. Now God can't use you unless you have peace! God had to give Gideon peace of mind. Now it's not the kind of peace you can presuppose. When God gives you peace, God has a propensity to give us peace in the midst of confusion! See some people think peace means I got money and everything is paid. No that's not peace, that's rest. God can give you peace and there can be chaos going on all around you. In your spirit and in your mind you don't have any anxiety because He says I will keep him in perfect peace whose mind is stayed on me. So you can lose your resource, but you don't have to lose your mind! You can get your car repossessed but you don't have to go crazy, because some of us, not all of us, know that God is our Source and if I lose my job I have something better coming! If I lose my house I got something better coming because I never trusted in my house. I never prayed to my house. I never prayed to my job, I never said come on and deliver me! My prayer has always been to God. So whatever happens he can keep me in perfect peace. All whose mind is stayed on thee. Even if you lose everything you have. Even if you get a pink slip tomorrow. "Oh, God I don't know how we're gonna eat." You're eating right now. But fear forecasts there's not going to be provision. I read in my Bible, do not misconstrue peace for provision because sometimes there is no provision but there is still peace. What if God said you are going to live like I had Israel live, on daily bread. People wouldn't make it. You pray that prayer, "Give us this day our daily bread." What if He only fed you with daily bread? There's no bread for next week, nothing in the freezer, nothing in the cupboard but every morning you wake up, every morning you rise, there is manna falling from heaven! People think they can't live like that. "I don't know if it's going to show up tomorrow, I need to try and save some of this." When you try to save some of it, it dissolves, when you tried to save it, worms came and ate it. He wasn't giving you leftovers, he had fresh bread, but only if you trust Him, you know He will deliver every single day.

So how are you having anxiety when they say the job is going to close in a year or two or three? And you're worried about something that may happen in the future. Your problem is your defence and your trust has been in your job. But for some of us we know that God is the One who gave us the promotion, God is the one who opened the door, God is the one who made the way, so I know how to feel the fear and trust God anyway!

So Gideon has peace and peace is not based on provision. Sometimes peace is your provision. Everybody else is up in arms about it and your home asleep. "You're not worried about that?" they say. "My cousin went through that, and they died." You can respond, "I'm not your cousin." Read your Bible, it says, "I am going to use you to deliver you out of the hands of the Midianites, and raise you up, my hand is on you, my hand is on you." But the first thing you have to do is tear down the groves of Baal. Gideon says, "I am going to do it but I am going to do it at night so they don't know it was me." So Gideon goes into the camp and destroys the groves of Baal, the false god and word gets out that somebody came in and destroyed the groves of Baal. Who do you think it was? And they started talking amidst each other and they draw the conclusion that they think it was Gideon. So Gideon gets busted out, they find out it was him and they send a letter to his father, Joash. Can we walk through the Bible? And they come to Joash's house and he says, "You've come to kill my son, because the letter says that your son has destroyed the groves of Baal. Because he has upset Baal, we've come to destroy your son." And Joash says, "You mean to tell me that your god got stopped by my boy? How bad is Baal that my son the least in my house the one we would never pick, he has crippled your god, and you've come to defend your god? Why can't your god defend himself?" And the Bible says their anger was abated. You jump down to the seventh verse and you'll see Jerubbaal, Jerubbaal, whose name is Gideon,

Judges 7:1, Then Jerubbaal, who is Gideon..

Now what happened between chapter 6 and chapter 7? I'm glad you asked. Jerubbaal is the name of the one who resisted Baal. They gave Gideon a nickname and when his name gets changed and all the people that were with him, rose up early, and pitched beside the well of Harod: so that the host of the Midianites were on the north side of them, by the hill of Moreh, in the valley.

Now when you read that you may not get a proper understanding so let's exegete the text. Now what happens here is Jerubbaal who is Gideon, his name has been changed, because he has challenged Baal. But the problem with some of us is that when God takes you to another level, some of the people who knew you by your old name don't identify with you now. Simply because you are not Gideon, because now God has stretched you and now you're on another level. You think being lonely is because people don't like you, and people don't want to be around you. Loneliness comes before promotion, see now the people who knew Gideon don't know him as Jerubbaal. And so when people only know you by what you used to be and don't know you by what you've become, they'll back away from you. So I am saying to everyone of you, having lonely weeks, and lonely months and a lonely year, I thank God because you need some of these people away from you! What precedes your promotion is your loneliness! So if you're lonely now look over your shoulder because in the midst of your loneliness, your promotion must be after you, because you will never be promoted without your season of loneliness. That's why you've got to feel the fear and do it anyway!

So now as Jerubbaal, they don't know who he is anyways because his name has been changed, and it's been changed without their cooperation and without their commitment. Then when his name is changed, God says go ahead and handle the Midianites. Well here is his problem, he is facing two kings. Now in the midst of this the Bible says, he gathered his men. He gathered 33,000 men. 33,000 to help him. And in Chapter 7 the Bible says, God says to him, "You've got to many people, less I deliver the Midianites into your hand, you'll think that you did it."

Why can't you get anybody to help you, why can't you get anybody to work with you? It's a God thing, it's God thing. Because if you get too many people involved, God won't get the glory, God won't get the credit. 33,000 - God says you've got too many. So God makes this statement, "Whoever is afraid, and fearful, let them go home." Next verse says, 22,000 men went home. You've had 33,000 working with you, 22,000 go home because they are afraid. There's a difference versus a crowd and a team. See a crowd is close together, but everybody has their own agenda. But a team works with one agenda, am I talking with anybody? That's why you gotta be careful who you are working with, that may be a crowd, not a team! Crowds flip, crowds boo, crowds cheer, crowds turn on you, but a team will be with you when the bottom drops out and your back is against the wall!

Everyone can go to the amateur night at the Apollo, and boo, boo, boo when you get on the stage. So don't get lost in all your numbers of your so called feigns, I mean friends. This is your crowd and your crowd is deceiving, you need a team. Gideon had gathered a crowd, 22,000 went home because they were scared and afraid. 11,000 are left and God said, "Gideon, you still have too many."

Now go down to the brook and I'll tell you who's with you and who isn't. He said those who go down to the brook and drink water on their knees, send them home. Those that drink water as a dog, lapping the water with their hands, keep them. Now when he says drink water like a dog, most people think that just means lick the water, but actually if you look at it in slow motion as I did, when a dog drinks water, his tongue cups and the water is on the back of his tongue, not the front. When he sticks his tongue in the water, his tongue curls and becomes a ladle. And it's a quick ladle for him to scoop up the water quickly. The man who laps like a dog, which means makes his hand a ladle, and drinks, keep him. So as a result 7,700 men are dismissed, 300 left. Facing 22,000. Gideon has some men with him who know how to drink and watch. You can't have anyone on your team who is going to lay down their weapon, say "I'm coming," get on their knees and slurp up the water, "I got thirsty," you're going to get us killed. You need people who know how to look and lap at the same time. The enemy is only 300 yards away, I can still drink, you need people who know how to watch. You can't be running with people who don't know how to watch. The Bible tells us we need to watch and pray. We need to have our eyes open. You can't be having a tent revival in the neighborhood, where there's more hoods than neighbors and there's a tent up and

IT'S A MATTER OF DOMINION

there's people there looking at your purse, looking at your material and your sitting there, you better keep your eyes open and be praying, "God, bless them, don't touch that, make a way out of no way."

I had a dog, my dog was named Princess Sandra Hennings, she was registered in Washington D.C., she's gone now, she's in doggy heaven. I'm keeping her there, I don't care what you say. One day I was watching a fight or something on TV, and I ordered a pizza. My wife, Pamela is a vegetarian, I am not. I am what's called an omnivore. An omnivore eats a little bit of everything. So my pizza had sausage, pepperoni, green peppers, mushrooms, and black olives if you don't mind, and extra cheese, well done. It's my pizza, I can enjoy it. So I am watching the program and I hear this noise of licking and eating. I know it's not me, so I put the TV on mute, and I am listening to this eating and slurping. My dog is eating all the topping off of my pizza. Now when I saw her she didn't run off, she looked at me and got her last few bites in. You need people who know how to look and eat at the same time. I said, "Sandy!" Now most dogs run away with their tail between their legs. My dog started creeping away, you can ask my wife. I said, "Sandy!" I could have sworn I heard her say, "Can you see me?" Just walking away slow, my dog taught me a lesson. I know I am going to get it so I am going to get all I can! Learn how to look and lap at the same time!

300 men, this is the same Gideon now, who was scared and apprehensive. He goes in after the Midianites and he comes across a

young man. He says to the young man, we've come to defeat the enemy and we're hungry. We need some vigilance, and on his way he comes across Ephraim and Ephraim says to him, "Why didn't you tell us you were going to battle?" You shouldn't have gone to battle without our help. He was not even known for being a fighter, but when God starts using you, people jump on your bandwagon. Now nobody asked to help him before. "When you go to battle, you should call us," they say. That's why people struggle when God starts promoting you without their influence. You'd be surprised by the people sitting with you in church. You've overlooked them for the last 5 years and don't even speak to them. You don't get along with them and you don't even know why. Most people struggle with other people because you see their potential and their not walking in it but you see it on them. Then what happens is God starts using them without your permission or without your influence on them and you say, "Well you should have called me!" That's what happened to Gideon, they say "Gideon, why didn't you call us?" And he says, "Well you're Ephraim, you all are big boys, I wasn't going to call you for this little job," and he squelches their anger, but then something strange happens. I am talking about feeling the fear and doing it anyway. You'd be surprised how many entrepreneurs are out there who will die with their entrepreneurism in the grave, because you're afraid of having five days of a growling stomach. Did I lose the amens? You're afraid to have a lean season, it's called equanimity-to stay calm and relaxed under pressure! It's the ability to laugh at things that are ridiculous and out of the ordinary. If you can't do that, God won't use you. I have heard people say things like, "I saw in a dream that the devil was going to kill you," I gotta call the prayer warriors together and you sit there and bind that buffoonery. No, God already had a plan for your life, and you have to have equanimity. You can say something like, "Is that what your dream was, because God just showed me we're going to the Bahamas next week."

Most people don't realize God doesn't want you to camp on the trip, he wants you to get to your destiny, and because things happen on the trip, people get stuck there. But the trip is not the destiny, it's where you are on the way to your destiny. Some people are a trip. Some people you have to get over so you can get to where you are supposed to be. That's why you should never give people the ability to press your buttons. I don't like that saying - they are pressing my buttons. I don't give people that much power that they can press my buttons and get me upset. I want to be in the place where I have strong consolation, what you said used to make me cry but now it's making me laugh. Consolation works because you can just start laughing. Even though they haven't said anything funny, you can start laughing, because strong consolation makes you laugh at the ridiculous and the absurd. You need to get to the place in God where what used to make you cry with tears coming down your face, now makes you laugh. This lets every demon know I feel the fear and I am going to do it anyway. You will know it's God because what used to make you cry now makes you laugh.

Now there is a cycle of repentance, it has four phases. The first phase is apostasy. Apostasy is the falling away. Now when you fall away, apostasy, we have in error misused the word apostasy and substituted it with backsliding. So when people walked away from God in the 21st century, we say, "Oh they backslid however, you can't backslide unless you're married. Let me prove it to you. To backslide, God says I am married to the backslider, to Israel. To backslide means to go forward or backward and still be connected. In other words, a married couple. A woman decides she is upset with her husband, and goes home to her parents, even if she goes home she is still married. But if they were dating and they called the wedding off, that's apostasy, a falling away. It's off. In church people don't backslide they fall away. Take for the sake of hypothesis a member of a congregation who sits on the front row, then the third row, then the fifth row. The next week she is on the 8th row and then the last row, next week she's in a rowboat, not in church at all. That's called apostasy, falling away. When people start becoming unfaithful to God and unfaithful to church, that's called apostasy. And people lie and say they had to work. That's a whole lot of work you are doing and you're giving hasn't changed. See you lie, because you don't have any accountability. Or someone sees you sand you say, "Oh I am coming back," but nobody said anything. People fall away, it's called apostasy. Somebody made you angry, there's apostasy in our music department. I had a meeting with 100 choir members, 100 members, 40 singing, 20 coming to rehearsal, that's called apostasy, a falling away, but you want the best of God, but you're falling away!

First step is apostasy, second step is servitude, because every time Israel fell away from God, God made them serve their enemy! When you fall away from God you go into servitude. In other words you go back to the world and the world did not embrace you like you thought it would. Because you're a dim light now. You don't go back on pause, press pause and go back to where you used to be now. When you left God they were doing the running man, now they doing something else and you don't fit in, you still doing the running man, so you're trying to fit in, but they don't want you there! You're messing up their high, they can't enjoy their drink, because you were hope to them! You had them convinced that the God you serve was able to do exceeding abundantly above all you're able to ask or think. And you were their hope, that one day they would be able to get it together, but then you show up with them and you kill their hope, they're not glad you came back, now you're dating people you said you'd never date, kissing people you said you'd never kiss. You got back your sensual clothes, got all that yesterday on! Looking worse than you did the first time, because it's called apostasy, you fall away and you don't have real people in your life to tell you how bad you look, because you look bad. Don't ever think you can leave God and do better, because there is nothing better than God. I don't care how it looks. Your worse day over here is better than your best day over there! I don't care who did you wrong or how you feel, you are on the right ship when you're in the church, the fellowship is the best ship to be on, but if you leave God, your best day in the world can't match your worst day in the kingdom!

David said my foot almost slipped when I saw the prosperity of the wicked, but then I got to the house of the Lord.

That's why when you start going through things, never back off from church, you want to be the first one there, shaking the doors. When does it open? Because I am going through something and I know my help in in God!

You've got people who don't have dreams. You have two kinds of people in church, dream killers and dream stealers. These people come to church just like the rest of us, every time you share something, they say "Oh that ain't gonna work." Stop sharing your dreams! Stop telling everybody what you want to do, because you had dream killers, they'll kill it. Then you have dream stealers, who will steal your idea and try to work it, but there's no anointing to do it, that's why it doesn't work for them! I have to tell you the truth, a dream stealer will take what you said, and try to use it for themselves, but because there's no oil on it, it won't work. Apostasy, falling away. Number two servitude, start doing things you thought you would never do. Step number three is supplication. That's when you say, God I am messed up. I don't know how I got out here...but God give me another chance, help! When you get to this spot you can forget about church people. They have already written you off. But you better thank God that he tarries until you come back! That's what he did for Gideon. He said, "Gideon I will wait for you until you get yourself together." So he gives you room to supplicate, when you say, "God I did it, please give me another chance." That's step number three.

Fourth step is salvation. That's when God answers your prayer, rescues you, and dips you in the blood, and gives you another chance. That's why you gotta be careful how you judge people. Because you don't know where you are in the cycle. Somebody might be in the state of apostasy, somebody might be in supplication, somebody might be in salvation, somebody might be in servitude. But believe me it's a cycle and everybody's going to have to deal with it, one way or another, and you gotta know how to feel the fear and do it anyway.

Let's just deal with the real issues. Some of us aren't living it. God is not into the noise, He is into the praise. He is not hearing your praise and receiving it if you don't have a life that is conducive to Him getting your praise!

The Bible says in Psalm 150 that everything that has breathe is to praise the Lord. Everything can praise Him but He doesn't respond to everything that praises Him! The real praises are the ones who God comes down in your praise and He stands in it. The Bible says, "Thou art holy, O Thou who inhabits the praise of His people." In other words when the real praisers praise God He steps in your praise, and lives in it! Now when you're just a noise maker, living any way and giving God praise, it's just noise. He doesn't step into noise, and live in noise but He does abide in praise. That's why I have to make sure when I am in this cycle of repentance I don't have time to look at your hand, I need to find where I am, because this is my trip, not my destiny. Everybody's going to have a bad day. Everybody's going to be in a bad mood one day, you're going to catch everybody with a funky disposition. But don't judge where I am in this cycle because I might be evolving into another level. Most people cannot get with you, because you have become something that you were not yesterday. "Well I remember him last year." Well that was last year, that is not who I am today. I remember her from five years ago. The old woman you knew is dead! The new woman of today you have not met, that's why when she saw you she walked right past you, because you are in her land of 'was," and you'll start looking at some people as your mistake and bad decision! That was my mistake, that was my bad decision, I was drunk, I was high, but now I am a brand new creature, and I am not going back to the land of "Was."

Now Gideon says I have come to deal with you king, the young boy says, "Who do you think you are?" You're from Manasseh, the least in your family. Gideon said not only am I going to conquer your kings, when I come back, I am going to tear your flesh off. This is Gideon, the one who was crying two chapters before, but when God anoints you He gives you power!

6 And the princes of Succoth said, Are the hands of Zebah and Zalmunna now in thine hand, that we should give bread unto thine army?

In other words, who do you think you are, you're going to come here and think you're going to defeat our king and you want us to feed you too? I remember you when you were in the 6th grade. That's what people do. People don't know what you've become, that's why they discount you. You'd be surprised how many people devalue you because they have no contribution to you've become! They'll make you feel that you haven't done anything because they weren't a part of your progress.

Take a look at verse 7,

7 And Gideon said, Therefore when the Lord hath delivered Zebah and Zalmunna into mine hand, then I will tear your flesh with the thorns of the wilderness and with briers.

This is the same Gideon who was apprehensive that God would use him. Now God has anointed him with such an anointing that he would feel the fear and do it anyway.

Not only is God going to deliver these kings to us, but I am going to come back and rip off your flesh. This is Gideon.

Verse 13 same chapter, And Gideon the son of Joash returned from battle before the sun was up.

This battle should have taken years, but this battle took minutes. The man went into battle with 300 and conquered 20,000 in minutes.

That's how you know God is with you. People have to admit that God is with you. They may not be able to stand you, but they'll still say, "I don't like them but I see God is with them."

13 And Gideon the son of Joash returned from battle before the sun was up,

In other words, "I'll be right back honey, I have to go to work."

14 And caught a young man of the men of Succoth, and enquired of him: and he described unto him the princes of Succoth, and the elders thereof, even threescore and seventeen men.

15 And he came unto the men of Succoth, and said, Behold Zebah and Zalmunna, with whom ye did upbraid me, saying, Are the hands of Zebah and Zalmunna now in thine hand, that we should give bread unto thy men that are weary?

16 And he took the elders of the city, and thorns of the wilderness and briers, and with them he taught the men of Succoth.

This is Gideon, the man with the inferiority complex.

6 And the princes of Succoth said, Are the hands of Zebah and Zalmunna now in thine hand, that we should give bread unto thine army?

7 And Gideon said, Therefore when the Lord hath delivered Zebah and Zalmunna into mine hand, then I will tear your flesh with the thorns of the wilderness and with briers.

"When I get done, I am coming back for you."

Verse 14...

14 And caught a young man of the men of Succoth, and enquired of him: and he described unto him the princes of Succoth, and the elders thereof, even threescore and seventeen men.

He said, get them all together.

15 And he came unto the men of Succoth, and said, Behold Zebah and Zalmunna, with whom ye did upbraid me, saying, Are the hands of Zebah and Zalmunna now in thine hand, that we should give bread unto thy men that are weary?

He was saying here are the guys you were giving me a hard time about, saying who do you think you are? Remember you said all that to me?

Verse 16...

16 And he took the elders of the city, and thorns of the wilderness and briers, and with them he taught the men of Succoth.

Didn't I tell you I was coming back? This is Gideon now. The same one that said, "Oh me? I am from a poor family and the least of my father's house."

Now he says, "I told you I was going to get the king didn't I?"

Yeah, yeah, I told you. Then because you tried to embarrass me and tell me I didn't have the authority, I told you I was going to come back and tear your skin off with thorns and briars. The God I serve is a God of deliverance, he delivered me and I am about to deliver you.

Some of you better quit crying when the enemy comes against you and take up your weapons. And tell every demon, "Didn't I tell you to leave my marriage alone? Didn't I tell you to leave my children alone?

Do I have any Gideons?

Feel the fear and do it anyway! Don't mess with people who are anointed. Don't mess with people God's got his hand on.

He beat them down so bad, look at verse 17...

17 And he beat down the tower of Penuel, and slew the men of the city.

Most people don't get this when he said he beat down. He beat them down. Not simply the tower, but they were giving praise until their praise became a tower, but he gave them a beatdown.

This is the same Gideon who in chapter 6 was apprehensive if God could use him. But then when God anoints him and gives him a name; he's not the same person. Likewise with you, you're not the same boy you used to know. You are not the same girl you used to know. Now I am God's man, now I am God's woman. That's why when you got to cry, you got to do it anyway. That's why you gotta be alone, do it anyway. You have to feel bad, feel bad and do it anyway.

The next chapter says the sword of the Lord and of Gideon! When he started out, he didn't even have a sword. Now folks start referring to him as the sword of the Lord and of Gideon. The sword of the Lord and the sword of (insert your name). Any time God uses you and you've been outnumbered but you still win, everybody has to admit, though they hate to admit, God had to do that. Because we all tried to mess her up, we all tried to hinder him, we all tried to lie on her. We all tried to jam him up. Do it anyway!

I read that Scripture and it changed the game. Feel the fear and do it anyway. Some people don't want to walk away from a bad relationship where they are living together, but aren't married. They don't know how to pay the bills, or make it. Feel the fear and do it anyway. God will give you peace in the midst of the storm.

I am going to show you how profound God is when he wants you to make it. Everywhere I go and I rent a car, I use Hertz. My prerequisite is a GPS. Hertz calls it, "never lost," and hence you're never lost. So I am driving and I don't care where I am, that Hertz GPS will say, "rerouting." I can never get lost! I learned something, if I trust God I may be late, but not lost! We were in Australia, riding around in a cart on a island. I didn't know where I was going. I got in the car to get back and I hit the never lost button. I made a wrong turn and it began rerouting. If I would have stopped where I was and broke down crying, I would have parked on my trip, even if I forget my way, my "never lost" will remind me of my destination! No matter what happens, everywhere I go, on the Santa Monica freeway, never lost is working. Sometimes it says lost satellite connection, so I just keep driving, no matter how far I go, it kicks back on and tells me where to go.

Now God called Gideon in chapter 6 and told him he was going to deliver Israel out of the hand of the Midianites, as one man. 33,000 men started with him, 22,000 left him. He had 10,000 men, out of the 10,000 men, 7,700 left and he had three hundred left. And they shouted, the sword of the Lord and of Gideon, as if he did it by himself. Sometimes when you get where you are going, they'll think you did it by yourself, but God navigated you the whole time. Anybody who has lost their keys, at the right time, God spared you from a car accident. Some of you couldn't find the things you were looking for, God spared you just to avoid something catastrophic, God is navigating you the whole time, so when you don't know what to do, feel the fear and do it anyway.

Let's pray.

Father, thank you that even when we are afraid, you are with us and working in us. Thank you that because you are with us, we can overcome our fears and serve you, whatever you are asking of us. Thank you for your grace that is all sufficient for all things. In Jesus' name. Amen.

"It's a Matter of Dominion!"

ABOUT BISHOP RODERICK L. HENNINGS

Bishop Roderick L. Hennings ~ a prolific speaker, renowned teacher, a powerful preacher, apologist, one used by the Holy Ghost to "change lives in an unchanging world". He is a lecturer, a coach, and a leadership mentor.

Roderick L. Hennings founded Zion Dominion Global Ministries in

1993. His unique ability to communicate the Word of God without compromise attracts people from different socioeconomic backgrounds; races and nationalities; and has caused a continued growth in membership from 20 at inception to currently over 4,000

Bishop Hennings continues to serve the International and Jurisdictional COGIC church in several capacities. On November 8, 2015 at the COGIC 18th Holy Convocation, Roderick L. Hennings was elevated to Bishop.

He was appointed COGIC Assistant White House Liaison in 2013 and Director of Church Growth & Development in January 2013. In 2014 Bishop Hennings was appointed an Administrative Assistant and District Superintendent to Bishop Glenwood H. Young Sr. Jurisdiction Prelate of New York Western Jurisdiction #2. Bishop Hennings has previously served as: Chairman of the Ordination Board of Jurisdiction #1, Administrative Assistant to Jurisdictional Prelate of New York Western Jurisdiction #1, International, COGIC Vice President of the Youth Department; International COGIC Executive Board Member of the Men's Department; and New York Western Jurisdiction #1 Institute Instructor.

In 2015 the RLH Hennings Midwest College was launched, offering Associate, Bachelor, Master and Doctoral Degrees. The R.L. Hennings Midwest College held its first graduation in July 2016 with over 80 graduating students from across the state of New York.

In addition to his faithfulness to ministry, Bishop Hennings has a strong commitment to the general community. He currently sits on the board of directors for the United Way. He has served as a Board member of Grace Manor Nursing Home; Chairman for Buffalo Affiliate of BLCA (Black Leadership Commission on AIDS); a committee member of the Western New York Leadership Summit; he collaborated with Hopevale, Inc. to offer faith based services for abused women and children; applied and received grant monies to purchase new computers to increase computer literacy among people in low income areas.

Bishop Hennings is a keen advocate of technology. Along with church Facebook and Twitter accounts, services at Zion Dominion are now streamed live from www.ziondominion.org. Services can also be heard on WUFO AM 1080 Radio, Buffalo NY every Wednesday morning. He has also been on The WORD Network as well as making guest appearances on TBN Church Praise ~ Los Angeles CA, and is a frequent guest of TCT Christian Television.

Roderick Hennings is the husband of one wife, First Lady Pamela D. Hennings and the father of his only two daughters: Ariane and Chloé Hennings.

Made in the USA
Middletown, DE
15 October 2017